About Access Archaeology

Access Archaeology offers a different publishing model for specialist academic material that might traditionally prove commercially unviable, perhaps due to its sheer extent or volume of colour content, or simply due to its relatively niche field of interest. This could apply, for example, to a PhD dissertation or a catalogue of archaeological data.

All *Access Archaeology* publications are available in open-access e-pdf format and in print format. The open-access model supports dissemination in areas of the world where budgets are more severely limited, and also allows individual academics from all over the world the opportunity to access the material privately, rather than relying solely on their university or public library. Print copies, nevertheless, remain available to individuals and institutions who need or prefer them.

The material is refereed and/or peer reviewed. Copy-editing takes place prior to submission of the work for publication and is the responsibility of the author. Academics who are able to supply print-ready material are not charged any fee to publish (including making the material available in open-access). In some instances the material is type-set in-house and in these cases a small charge is passed on for layout work.

Our principal effort goes into promoting the material, both in open-access and print, where *Access Archaeology* books get the same level of attention as all of our publications which are marketed through e-alerts, print catalogues, displays at academic conferences, and are supported by professional distribution worldwide.

Open-access allows for greater dissemination of academic work than traditional print models could ever hope to support. It is common for an open-access e-pdf to be downloaded hundreds or sometimes thousands of times when it first appears on our website. Print sales of such specialist material would take years to match this figure, if indeed they ever would.

This model may well evolve over time, but its ambition will always remain to publish archaeological material that would prove commercially unviable in traditional publishing models, without passing the expense on to the academic (author or reader).

Perspectives on materiality in ancient Egypt – agency, cultural reproduction and change

edited by

Érika Maynart, Carolina Velloza
and Rennan Lemos

Access Archaeology

Archaeopress Publishing Ltd
Summertown Pavilion
18-24 Middle Way
Summertown
Oxford OX2 7LG

www.archaeopress.com

ISBN 978 1 78491 933 7
ISBN 978 1 78491 934 4 (e-Pdf)

© Archaeopress and the individual authors 2018

Cover: "Taweret amulets from the cemetery of Fadrus, Lower Nubia".
Photo by Rennan Lemos. Courtesy of the Gustavianum Museum, Uppsala.

Printed and bound in Great Britain by
Marston Book Services Ltd, Oxfordshire

All rights reserved. No part of this book may be reproduced or transmitted, in any form or by any means, electronic, mechanical, photocopying or otherwise, without the prior written permission of the copyright owners.

Contents

Foreword iii

Editors' Foreword iv

Divine worship and action: representations of the Amarna Royal Family 1
Gisela Chapot

Children and materiality in Ancient Egypt 10
Benjamin Hinson

Materiality and cultural reproduction in non-elite cemeteries 24
Rennan Lemos

The sap of life: materiality and sex in the divine birth legend of Hatshepsut and Amenhotep III 35
Uroš Matić

Texts, materiality and agency in Middle Kingdom literature 55
Érika Maynart

"All that glitters is not gold": the symbolism and materiality of Egyptian funerary amulets 64
Carmen Muñoz Pérez

Materiality and history: some reflections 74
Marcelo Rede

The acting image and the materialisation of social realities 87
Carolina Velloza

Agency and representation of Nubians in Egyptian iconography in the 18th Dynasty:
ethnic strategies and negotiations 99
Fábio Amorim Vieira

The authors 110

Foreword

It is a great honour for me as president of the Association for Students of Egyptology to write the foreword to the volume Perspectives on materiality in ancient Egypt – agency, cultural reproduction and change. I cannot express how proud I am of the team who organised such a wonderful publication. The initial idea to discuss the subject took place in the form of a colloquium organised at the University of São Paulo in 2016—the very first event of the Association for Students of Egyptology. Unfortunately, time and money do not always allow everyone to be present at every event they would like, but thankfully the Internet serves as a bridge between different students all over the world. However, it is the combined time and effort of several students that make sure this bridge is used and maintained as well as possible, by publishing the results of their academic endeavours, which ASE is proud to support. This publication in particular has benefited from the network provided by ASE. The publication congregates students who firstly attempted to discuss 'materiality' in São Paulo, as well as other people engaged in the same discussions, who contributed with their ideas and papers to the present volume. Together with such a wonderful group of students and early career scholars, the ASE has the possibility to bridge the gap even further, so that time and travel play no more role in the communication, interaction, sharing of information and collaboration with each other. No matter how far you live, and whether your university has played a traditional role in Egyptology or not, everyone at the ASE is welcome to join and to collaborate; it is our passion for Egyptology and our academic mind-set that brings us all together.

Once more, I would like to congratulate Rennan, Érika and Carolina for organising such a successful publication. Mabrouk!

Lonneke Delpeut, president of the Association for Students of Egyptology

Editors' Foreword

Oswald de Andrade's 1925 poem ("Erro de Português", or Portuguese Mistake) depicts the first encounter between the Portuguese and Native Brazilians in the New World. The poet ironically narrates an encounter rich in nuances. He regrets that the Portuguese colonisers reached the land on a rainy day, which made them assume it was appropriate if they dressed the Natives. "What a pity!"—Andrade regrets. Had the Portuguese arrived on a sunny morning, the Natives would have undressed them!

Andrade's poem served as a source of inspiration for us when we organised the colloquium Perspectives on materiality in ancient Egypt – agency, cultural reproduction and change in 2016 in São Paulo—the first step towards the publication of these papers. This is a book conceived and mainly composed by Brazilian young scholars. It reflects the interests of people involved in research projects in departments of archaeology and history, but with a wider anthropological and theoretical interest within the humanities. We have explored our not-so-traditional place when it comes to Egyptological studies to propose discussions that—we hope—will be of interest to a broader audience among social scientists. Here we explore the metaphor of the Natives' potential of showing other perspectives to those who come from a different place, rich in longstanding traditions.

The papers presented here reflect the topics the editors considered fruitful to be discussed in the São Paulo colloquium. Nevertheless, we were fortunate enough to have the collaboration of colleagues from the 'Old World' who sent their contributions to our local discussions, mainly exploring topics we failed to develop further. The contact between us in a not-so-traditional residence and colleagues from well-established institutions proved to be extremely valuable in terms of exploring new directions from where knowledge is built and transferred across the world. New publications are increasingly showing that Egyptological knowledge can be produced from alternative, local—but interconnected—epistemological frameworks. Such frameworks may produce innovative perspectives that hold the potential of contributing to overcoming disciplinary challenges, already addressed in the literature. At the same time the present publication benefits from the traditional course of knowledge production from Europe towards the rest of the world, it also aims to progressively place the knowledge produced in the global south in the Egyptological mainstream. It requires from us the effort of continuously building bridges that carry the potential of assisting people from all around the world and producing other ways of looking at ancient Egyptian data in a way that may contribute to broader discussions.

The articles presented here may be understood as the result of our effort to build Egyptological bridges worldwide in order to create networks of collaboration from which new, interesting perspectives may come out. We have profited enormously from the network provided by the Association for Students of Egyptology, and we hope this publication boosts other efforts that bring together young scholars from different places to create original collaborations that can contribute to the renovation of theory and practice in Egyptology—a movement from which all will benefit, independently of their background.

Divine worship and action: representations of the Amarna Royal Family

Gisela Chapot

Introduction

During the Amarna Period, a process of solarisation of the religion influenced a new way of representing agents in Egyptian art. This is especially the case when members of the Royal Family are depicted as protagonists. The present contribution summarises the results of our PhD dissertation (Chapot 2015).

The image *corpus* upon which my analysis is based includes a group of 75 representations of the royal family, where the pharaoh Akhenaten, queen Nefertiti, and their six daughters perform various roles under the life-giving rays of the Aten. The scenes were organised into the following groups based on a thematic criterion: (1) cult scenes; (2) scenes of intimacy; (3) public appearances; and (4) reception of foreign tribute. A heterogeneous category identified as 'other appearances' also gathers images that did not fit in the previous groups. All groups include reliefs from temples, private tombs, the royal tomb, as well as elite houses and the boundary stelae.

The cult scenes: description and iconographic analysis

Scenes depicting the Royal Family in cultic activities are the most prominent type of artistic representation produced in the Amarna Period. Cult scenes comprise thirty-eight images in our catalogue. In this paper, I present an analysis of such scenes, emphasising the performance of the royal family in the Aten cult, as well as their interaction with the Sun Disc as the god's divine intermediaries various in religious contexts.

Cult scenes from other contexts in Egypt, such as the temple of Sety I at Abydos, provide evidence for reconstructing the daily ritual conducted in New Kingdom temples. In several scenes, the statue of the god is the main focal point. During the rituals conducted at Abydos, the god was awakened, greeted, washed, dressed, attired, fed, and purified (cf. David 1981). Nevertheless, at Amarna, it is a difficult task to reconstruct the ritual steps of the cult of the Aten. However, the ritual appears to have been centred in the act of offering, which included flowers, resin and braziers. This is attested, for instance, in the main building of the Great Aten Temple, where an endless number of offering tables located both inside and outside the building has been excavated (Kemp 2012, 90–91; Blackman 1922, 520). The elements used as offerings to the Aten were placed on top of these offering tables, which appear in several depictions in the tombs of Akhenaten's officials.

One of the main features that characterise religious ritual at Amarna is the avoidance of cult statues. Therefore, one might assume that the presentation of the usual offerings was unnecessary. In the cult scenes, lotus flowers, incense burners, water jugs, and ointments vessels are the main objects used by the Royal Family as offerings to the Aten (cf. Spieser 2010). Akhenaten and Nefertiti are usually positioned with their arms raised in worship, or bent before the god. Their daughters are seen usually rattling the sistrum, which was used during the liturgy and have strongly associations with the goddess Hathor (Manniche 2010, 15).

Another characteristic of the Amarna cult scenes is the prominent role played by women as substitutes of the goddess Hathor, especially Nefertiti. Lana Troy (Troy 1986, 127) and Lise Manniche (2010, 19) have previously discussed the so-called "hathorification" of Nefertiti. However, this idea has been well developed recently by Williamson based on her analysis of reliefs from Kom el-Nana. The interpretation claims that the Kom el-Nana was the Sunshade of Nefertiti. There, the queen was represented worshipping the Aten, acting like Hathor, and showing her ability as a creator goddess, but also as substitute of other goddesses in the religion of Amarna. According to those reconstructed scenes, it is possible that the Sunshade of the Queen was dedicated to aspects of herself associated with "cosmogonical aspects of queenship", and was a place of reunion of male and female elements (Williamson 2009, 446–447).

When expanding the scope of analysis beyond the cult scenes, the Amarna royal women might have also played a divine role in fertility private cults (Arnold 1996, 96–105; Stevens 2004, 124–125). Yet difficult to confirm, this assumption would corroborate the view that considers Nefertiti and her daughters as fulfilling the role of the goddess Hathor in cult scenes. One might interpret theirs as an indispensable role that supported cosmic maintenance according to Akhenaten's worldview.

Considering the cult scenes from the Theban period of Akhenaten's reign, one observes a clear distinction from what is later seen at Amarna. This is especially true for representations of Nefertiti, which are more fluid and varies more if compared with representations of Akhenaten himself. The pharaoh was depicted following a more restricted standard. In these scenes Akhenaten appears as the one who conducts the ritual in much higher proportions than Nefertiti. The only exception is the *sn-t3* or "kissing the ground" scenes, where she appears more prominently than him as officiating the cult (Vergnieux and Gondran 1997, 170–171).

Figure 1: the royal couple worshiping the sun. Luxor Museum. Photo courtesy of A. Brancaglion.

In figure 1, the king bears 'body cartouches' (Williamson 2009, 13). Williamson points to the fact that, when in the presence of the king at Thebes, the queen was never portrayed bearing body cartouches. Only when depicted alone Nefertiti would gain such distinctive traits in Theban ritual contexts, which Williamson believes is a "means of identifying the chief officiant/priest/priestess of the cult"

(Williamson 2009, 40). Thus, is possible that the building of Nefertiti's pillared hall intended to expose the queen wearing body cartouches, so Aton would recognise her also as an officiant, without overshadowing the authority of Akhenaten at Thebes (Williamson 2009, 209). At Amarna, body cartouches became more common, with the queen being depicted wearing them also when she stood besides the pharaoh. Also, they were not restricted to the temple anymore, which Williamson believes to be related to a more active aspect of the cult carried out at Amarna (Williamson 2009, 199).

I believe that this means that Nefertiti shares Akhenaten's religious status in ritual contexts at Amarna. The use of body cartouches could be also associated with a deification project of the royal couple in life. They were a distinctive feature of the royal couple as responsible for the cult of the Aten. At the same time, they might be interpreted as the embodiment of the consubstantial essence of the relationship between the Aten and royal couple, the only figures touched by the Sun's rays in this group of scenes.

In the cult scenes, the queen is depicted wearing a profusion of crowns and wigs. A common type of headdress worn by Nefertiti is the Hathor crown. As discussed before, it may be interpreted as a female deification element necessary in Akhenaten's worldview. In those scenes, Nefertiti may be associated with Hathor the "eye of Re"—an essential "feminine principle" for the world to gain form and to be constantly regenerated. Akhenaten and Nefertiti's daughters share the same role in the ritual landscape of Amarna, like in the scenes where they hold sistra (Troy 1986, 89–91).

The only daughter portrayed in the cult scenes at Thebes is Meritaten. She usually appears shaking a sistrum alongside Nefertiti. The princess wears similar clothes to the mother, though depicted with the side look and hairstyle typical of childhood.

The cult scenes at Amarna come from a variety of contexts beyond that of the Aten temples. For instance, a series of balustrade reliefs coming from the Great Palace indicate that Akhenaten used new architectural elements in the context of implementation of the new cult (Shaw 1994, 115–116).

The balustrades from religious and royal buildings at Amarna depict the royal couple and Meritaten. The pharaoh is shown alternating types of crowns, while the usual outfit consists of a skirt from which a bull's tail hangs. Nefertiti appears twice wearing a *khat*, though always dressed in a transparent pleated outfit. Although the balustrades are structurally identical, the actions undertaken by the royal family in the balustrade depictions are diverse. They include scenes of libation, consecration, and ointment presentation. It is interesting to observe that Nefertiti always repeats the gesture of Akhenaten and uses the same ceremonial devices as the king. It would indicate that both Akhenaten and Nefertiti's actions have the same ritual purpose and efficacy.

Another element that stands out in the balustrade reliefs is the difference in size between the king and the queen. This discrepancy may be related not only to the period in which the reliefs were made, as suggested by Williamson (2009, 206–207). Rather, it might indicate a connection with the place where they were erected. Therefore, the scenes carved in balustrades at the Great Palace would have been strictly linked with the display of royal power (see Freed et al. 1999, 152).

In boundary stelae R (Davies 1908, XLII), N (Davies 1908, XXXIII), S (Davies 1908, XXXIX) and A (Vergnieux and Gondran, 1997, 189). Akhenaten is shown wearing the *kheperesh* crown and a short kilt, from which hangs a bull tail. Nefertiti, on the other hand, wears a different crown in each of the scenes. Among the crowns worn by her is the Hathor crown, the iconic tall blue crown, another type of crown adorned with curved ram horns, and a crown decorated with tall feathers. In the boundary stelae scenes Maritaten and Meketaten also appear along the royal couple. I suggest that it might be related with the symbolism of number four, which denotes a notion of perfection and wholeness in Egyptian liturgy (cf.

Wilkinson 1994, 133).

Akhenaten and Nefertiti perform the same actions in the boundary stelae depictions. Both are represented with their arms raised in worship of the Aten. The emphasis on the act of worshipping is probably associated with the public placement of these images. These representations possibly enhance the role of the royal family as intermediaries between men and the Aten.

In the royal tomb Nefertiti also repeats Akhenaten's ritual actions. They are shown presenting lotus flowers, consecrating offerings and worshipping the Aten. The classic scene of the couple been flooded by solar rays in room alpha is clearly a visual expression of the hymns to Aten, with animals rejoicing in the light of the sun, which clearly emerges from the horizon (Martin 1989, plate XXXIV). Although we cannot see what the queen carries in her hands, it is possible that she is performing the same act of consecration of offerings as Akhenaten. The royal tomb was a place for solar regeneration whose rays emanated for the whole city of Amarna as source of all life. (Mallison 1999, 78).

In private tombs representations of the royal couple show a variation in the sizes of Akhenaten and Nefertiti. On the other hand they are depicted in a closer way, and their acts are performed in a more synchronised manner before the offering tables. For instance, figure 2 shows that the artist depicted Akhenaten and Nefertiti using a single contour. It indicates that both were represented in the same size, wearing the equivalent garments and crowns, and performing the same actions, e.g. spreading scented crystals in the Great Aten Temple. The idea that lies behind is that of the equivalence between the couple's actions in religious contexts.

Figure 2: the royal couple making offerings in the Great Aten Temple. Drawing by F. A. Vieira after Davies: 1905, plate XVIII.

In most of the cult scenes, the offerings were placed over a throne-altar containing the names of Aten, the king, and the queen in cartouches on its base. In some cases, the offerings were placed on frusto-conical offerings tables. Both types of offering tables also appear simultaneously, usually filled with lotus flowers and libation jars. Incense is burnt over the common offering set containing water jugs, round breads, vegetables, fruits, poultry, meat and flowers. This organisation of offerings has been interpreted as carrying a cosmogonical symbolism. According to Spieser, this symbolism expresses a tripartite ordering of the world: water, which refers to the primeval waters; the bread, in the middle, functioned as a "transition zone"; while the animals and plants, represented the terrestrial sphere (Spieser 2010, 27–28). The divine realm is represented by perfumes, lotus flowers and incense on the top, next to Aten.

Based on this interpretation, the presence of Aten on the offering tables might be seen as emphasising the continuous action of creation and re-creation of the universe, which was repeated each time the Aten shows itself on the horizon. Therefore, the excessive amount of provisions offered to the god serves as sustenance for the god to fulfil his function as maintainer of all life, including of the deceased in their tombs (Hornung 1999, 96).

Akhenaten is shown wearing the *kheperesh* crown in most of the cult scenes. The crown is associated with the reigning monarch (Collier 1996, 123–124) bearing no ties with any specific deity – e.g. neutral from a theological point of view. The same can be said about Nefertiti's iconic tall blue crown. This characteristic of the cult scenes matches the earlier proclamation text on the boundary stelae, which says that Akhenaten founded Akhetaten "when it did not belong to a god, nor to a goddess; when it did not belong to a male ruler, nor to a female ruler…" (Murnane 1995, 75).

In terms of performance, Akhenaten is most commonly shown burning scented crystals with a stick over the filled offering tables, which can be considered an innovation of the cult of the Aten (Spieser 2010, 82). This is common feature in cult scenes in private tombs, but also appears as in a domestic shrine in the official house of Panehesy in the Central City (Kemp 2012, 232). Nefertiti, on the other hand, only performs such an action in figure 2, where Akhenaten and Nefertiti are shown overlapped. The almost exclusivity of Akhenaten as the responsible for burning scented crystals in cult scenes leads us to believe that this is a crucial step in the daily ritual. In the same scenes, Nefertiti usually uses a *kherep* stick to consecrate offerings, and also holds a bowl with incense. It expresses the queen's role in the ritual assisting Akhenaten, as shown in the tomb of Mahu (Davies 1906, plate XV).

Purification is a key element in the cult scenes of the Amarna Period (Spieser 2010, 20–23). It is attested in the widespread depiction of the acts of burning incense and making libations. In the tomb of Panehesy, for instance, Akhenaten and Nefertiti appear using a censer and a *nmst* vase. The king leads the ritual with a *nmst* vase with the feather of Maat, which reinforces the purifying nature of the act (Davies 1905, plate V). In the Amarna Period, the concept of *maat* is associated with Akhenaten, the one who is "living in *maat*" (Assmann 2013, 82). Actually, the entire family contributed to the principle of *maat* personifying the cosmic order, not only Akhenaten (Vergnieux 2013, 90).

The image *corpus* from Amarna allows us to observe the close link between divine worship and the political and religious importance that Nefertiti acquired during the Akhenaten's reign. This process begun at Thebes and was completed at Amarna, where Nefertiti started to play an active role in the worship of the Aten, wearing garments and headdresses typically associated with the pharaoh.

The princesses do not appear in most of the available cult scenes. When they appear, only the older princesses are depicted, usually shaking the sistrum. Although secondary, they play a clear role in the liturgy, evoking the female element associated with Nefertiti and Hathor that has been suggested to be important in the Amarna worldview. Meritaten is shown performing a different movement than her sisters. In figure 2, Meritaten is depicted holding a bowl next to the royal couple. In the tomb of Tutu (Davies 1908, XVI) the princess is carrying a sceptre with an ostrich feather and a band named *sw*.

These are typical official attributes, which award prestige to the princess (Spieser 2010, 93).

The Aten appears in all cult scenes as the solar disk with rays ending in hands touching the offerings and the royal couple. An exception is found in the tomb of Meryra I where semicircles have been drawn below the sun disk (Davies 1903, plate XXII). Scholars have not reached consensus in the explanation of the symbolism of such a representation (Laboury 2010, 19). One point that deserves attention is that all actions performed by the royal family focuses the Aten, with no interaction among the family members.

The formal iconic units (cf. Bérard 1983) in the Amarna cult scenes are Akhenaten and Nefertiti, their daughters, the Aten, and the filled offering tables. Those comprise the basic iconographic repertoire, where the royal family carry an intermediate role between the Aten and the material world. The depicted officiating actions performed by the royal couple produce a reaction in the representation of the Aten, who thenceforth emanates light towards the royal family (figure 3). Subsequently, the royal family extends the blessings to the Egyptians, who should venerate Akhenaten and Nefertiti as living gods. It is the responsive reaction of the Aten towards the royal family's actions that enables the divine aspect of the royal couple.

Figure 3: Akhenaten and Nefertiti displaying the didactic name of the Aten. Drawing by F. A. Vieira after Davies: 1906, plate XXXI.

Conclusion

Superimposition of images was an uncommon feature in ancient Egyptian art. Artists prioritized the visibility of all elements that composed the scene (Robins 1986, 11–12). During the Amarna Period, the images of Akhenaten and Nefertiti overlap in some occasions. Their same sizes emphasise the oneness of the couple, and their consubstantiality with Aten.

In most of the cult scenes, a strong inclination towards the idea of purification can be identified. The steps of the daily ritual of the Aten include offerings of water, incense, and scented crystals. In other words, there is emphasis on acts of purity, which is also reflected in the white linen garments used by the royal family (Spieser 2010, 91). The purity of the ritual and the royal couple would emphasise their divinity. Their continuous representation as burning incense would also have connotations of purity, for the word *senetjer* (incense) means "to become divine" (Wilkinson 1994, 92–93).

Other divine traits of the royal couple can be identified. For instance, the rays of Aten only touch Akhenaten and Nefertiti. Also, only the royal couple are portrayed with body *cartouches* containing the names of the Aten; or only them are to use ribbons hanging from their crowns, an element which evoke the divine. The crowns worn by Akhenaten and Nefertiti are preferably the *kheperesh* and the tall blue crown, as they might be considered pure from the theological point of view as discussed.

The different elements present in the cult scenes described above, when considered together, create an iconographic identity for Akhenaten and Nefertiti. Androgynous traits, characteristic of the divinities Shu and Tefnut, were initially considered decisive to sustain Akhenaten's religious claims. In the second half of the reign, however, the humanisation of royal forms confirmed a new solar worldview. The definitive establishment of such an iconographic identity is the "deified" style of Akhenaten and Nefertiti, in same the way representations of the jubilee of Amenhotep III have been interpreted (Laboury 2010,10).

It should be noted, however, that the Amarna artistic representations do not conform a sort of realism. Egyptian art remained conceptual in the Amarna Period. Humanised representations of the royal couple made their divine aspect more accessible to individuals in order to be "placed in the heart" of their subjects. It consists of a reinforcement of the new relationship of indirect personal piety established in the Amarna Period, when the royal family should be worshiped for the purpose of provide the light of the Aten to their subjects (Assmann 2001, 216–217).

The cult scenes provide us basis for realising that, during the Amarna Period, the representations of Akhenaten, Nefertiti and their daughters maintained somehow the divine hierarchies found before in Egyptian religion. The divine hierarchies were reproduced within the royal family: Akhenaten and Nefertiti acted as great gods, while their daughters fulfilled the roles of minor gods. The deification of the royal family seems to have been crucial to support the new worldview, in which Akhenaten and Nefertiti were the main actors.

References

Arnold, D. 1996. **The Royal Women of Amarna. Images of Beauty from Ancient** Egypt. New York.

Assmann, J. 2001. **The Search for God in Ancient Egypt**. Ithaca: Cornell University Press.

Assmann, J. 2013. A new state theology. In F. Seyfried ed. **In the light of Amarna: 100 years of the Nefertiti discovery**. Berlin: Inhof Verlag, 79–83.

Berárd, C. 1983. Iconographie-Iconologie-Iconologique. **Éttudes de Lettres**, 4, 5–37.

Blackman, A. 1922. A Study of the Liturgy Celebrated in the Temple of the Aton at El-Amarna. In **Recueil D'études égyptologiques dédiées à la mémoire de Jean-François Champolion**. Paris: E. Champion, 505–527.

Chapot, G. 2015. **A Família Real Amarniana e a Construção de Uma Nova Visão de Mundo Durante o Reinado de Akhenaton**. Unpublished PhD Dissertation. Niterói: Universidade Federal Fluminense.

Collier, S. 1996. **The crowns of the pharaoh: their development and significance in ancient Egyptian kingship**. Unpublished PhD dissertation. Los Angeles: UCLA.

David, R. 1981. **A guide to religious ritual at Abydos.** Warminster: Aris & Phillips, 1981.

Davies, N. G. 1903. **The rock tombs of el-Amarna I**. London: Egypt Exploration Fund

Davies, N. G. 1905. **The rock tombs of el-Amarna II**. London: Egypt Exploration Fund.

Davies, N. G. 1906. **The rock tombs of el-Amarna IV**. London: Egypt Exploration Fund.

Davies, N. G. 1908. **The rock tombs of el-Amarna V**. London: Egypt Exploration Fund.

Davies, N. G. 1908. **The rock tombs of el-Amarna VI**. London: Egypt Exploration Fund.

Freed, R., Y. Markowitz and S. D'Auria eds. 1999. **Pharaohs of the Sun: Akhenaten, Nefertiti, Tutankhamen**. London: Thames and Hudson.

Hornung, E. 1999. **Akhenaten and the religion of light**. Ithaca: Cornell University Press.

Kemp, B. J. 2012. **The city of Akhenaten and Nefertiti: Amarna and its people**. London: Thames and Hudson.

Laboury, D. 2010. **Akhenáton**. Paris: Pygmalion edition.

Mallinson, M. 1999. The sacred landscape. In R. Freed, Y Markowitz and S. D'Auria eds. **Pharaohs of the Sun: Akhenaten, Nefertiti, Tutankhamen**. London: Thames and Hudson, 72–79.

Manniche, L. 2010. The Cult Significance of the Sistrum in the Amarna Period. In A. Woods, A. McFarlane, and S. Binder eds. **Egyptian Culture and Society. Studies in Honor of Naguib Kanawati**. Vol. 2. Cairo: Supreme Council of Antiquities, 13–26.

Martin, G. T. 1989. **The Royal Tomb at El-'Amarna. II: The Reliefs, Inscriptions and Architecture**. London: Egypt Exploration Society.

Murnane, W. 1995. **Texts from the Amarna Period in Egypt**. Atlanta: Scholars Press.

Robins, G. 1986. **Egyptian painting and relief**. Aylesbury: Shire Egyptology.

Shaw, I. 1994. Balustrades, stairs and altars in the cult of the cult of the Aten at el-Amarna. **Journal of Egyptian Archaeology** 80, 109–127.

Spieser, C. 2010. **Offrandes et purification à l'époque amarnienne**. Turnhout: Brepols.

Stevens, A. 2004. The Amarna royal women as images of fertility: perspectives on a royal cult. **Journal of Ancient Near Eastern Religions**, 4, 107–127.

Troy, L. 1986. **Patterns of Queenship in Ancient Egyptian Myth and History**. Uppsala: Uppsala

University (Acta Universitatis Upsaliensis).

Vergnieux, R. 2013. Akhet-Aten or the Horizon of the Aten: an innovation in sacred architecture. In F. Seyfried ed. **In the light of Amarna: 100 years of the Nefertiti discovery**. Berlin: Inhof Verlag, 84–91.

Vergnieux, R and M. Gondran. 1997. **Aménophis IV et les pierres du soleil: Akhénaton retrouvé**. Paris: Arthaud.

Williamson, J. 2009. **Reconstruction and identity of Kom el-Nana at Tell el-Amarna: an analysis of decorated stone fragments from Kom el-Nana, and the role of the structures called "Sunshades of Re" in the Amarna Period**. Unpublished PhD Dissertation. Baltimore: Johns Hopkins University.

Wilkinson, R. 1994. **Symbol and Magic in Egyptian Art**. London: Thames & Hudson.

Children and materiality in Ancient Egypt

Benjamin Hinson

Introduction

The presence of children is one of few commonalities linking societies past and present. Children are estimated to have formed at least half of most ancient populations (Hiner and Hawes 1985, 14; Chamberlain 1997, 250, 2000; Grimm 2000, 53; Hutson 2006, 104). Although few demographic approximations exist, there is no reason to believe differently of Pharaonic Egypt. Estimates of household size at Deir el-Medina suggest that the average family had 2-3 children at any time (Valbelle 1985, 84; Koltsida 2007, 12), with as many as 6-8 offspring surviving to adulthood (Lesko 1994, 6; Kemp 2005, 157).

However, the prevalence of children in Egyptian society is not mirrored by an ease in finding their material traces. Discussing the materiality of children in ancient Egypt is fraught with problems. It is only in recent centuries that a discrete 'material culture' of childhood has emerged, such as purpose-made toys. This is not to say that children in the past did not engage with material. Rather, they engaged with the same material world as the rest of society. However, archaeological discussion of children's materiality has consistently been influenced by modern Western ideas of childhood. Most frequently, material is assumed to be associated with children because of its size or crudeness, and visual similarities to modern toys, but other misconceptions also persist.

Although recognised elsewhere in archaeology (Sofaer Derevenski 2000; Harlow 2013; Dozier 2016), these issues have received little treatment within Egyptology. This paper therefore outlines problems surrounding the discussion of children's materiality in ancient Egypt, alongside other theoretical considerations. It aims to present both a more nuanced approach to studying children's materiality, and avenues for future research in this area.

Child and childhood in Ancient Egypt

Before beginning analysis, 'childhood' requires discussion. Physically being a child, and the growth of the body, is a universal human experience. However, 'childhood' is more than this. It is "the package of experiences, attitudes, perceptions, expectations and provisions which are specific to the immature human and which derive from the way in which it is considered different from the mature adult" (Crawford and Lewis 2009, 7–8). In other words, childhood is socially constructed, and therefore unique to specific socio-cultural contexts (James 1998; James and Prout 1990; James, Jenks and Prout 1998; Prout 1999). The points at which childhood is considered to begin and end, and the treatment of individuals of different ages, are culturally situated. Being culturally specific, it cannot even be assumed that a distinct condition of 'childhood' actually exists in every culture. Nor is childhood homogenous within a society; an individual's experience might differ depending on class, gender, or even developmental capabilities.

Modern ideas of childhood as a time of innocence and leisure emerged only in recent centuries, with technological changes and the growth of the middle-classes lessening the need for children to play an economic role. Our understanding of childhood, as a period primarily of recreation, is therefore only meaningful in relation to modern Western culture. It is inapplicable to most past and many modern societies, where children contribute economically from a young age (Nieuwenhuys 1996). Furthermore, 'child' as employed in modern English is itself a broad term, encompassing a wide range of developmental stages, again reflecting modern Western notions of structuring the life-course (Sofaer Derevenski 1997, 193; Kamp 2001, 3; Baxter 2005, 96).

When discussing the materiality of children in ancient Egypt, therefore, 'childhood' must be understood in reference to ancient Egyptian understandings. There has been limited research into this area, or even Egyptian concepts of the life-course more generally (though see Meskell 2000). The Egyptians had a concept of a lifetime, the ꜥḥꜥw ('standing'). Each individual accumulated experiences and traits throughout life, which were used to judge their fate upon death. There are also indications that this journey was considered to contain discrete parts. Several statue groups depict the same individual at different stages of life (Peck 1978, 73), each depiction 'representing' a particular stage. Certain texts, such as the Inscription of Bakehnkhonsu (Munich Gl.WAF 38), also delineate periods of life. However, these sources cannot be assumed to reflect generally-held conceptions. The parameters described in different sources vary, and texts especially may primarily reflect the authors' biases and intentions rather than societal norms. By way of parallel, Classical authors also discussed divisions within the lifecycle, typically describing stages of four, seven or nine years. However, rather than reflecting social attitudes, such divisions were poetic, influenced by superstition, astrology, magic or the 'Four Ages of Rome' (Eyben 1973, 150–90; Parkin 2010, 97–9). The specifics of 'progression' through the Egyptian life-cycle are therefore poorly understood.

However, the Egyptians did have some concept of a childhood. Mortuary art indicates broad distinctions between 'adult' and 'non-adult', although with little nuance. Possibly, this reflects reality and a limited interest in delineating the life-cycle; conversely, it could reflect only the contexts of such evidence. By contrast, there are many words attested as referring to non-adults. Although these are typically all translated as 'child', they likely had specific nuances (Hinson 2017). However, it is unclear whether these reflect different stages of childhood, different registers of language, or different contexts or use—nor is it clear how the use of vocabulary overlapped in time.

In short, adult and non-adult were distinguished in ancient Egypt. However, how they were differentiated, and when the threshold was passed, are not yet fully understood, nor whether further stages were marked within this. It is possible that understandings of childhood varied by context and even class (Marshall 2015, 52), and also across time. Egyptian civilisation covered a vast geographical and temporal scope; variation between periods and even on a regional level might all be expected. More nuanced analysis is needed to clarify these issues.

Children and materiality

Although childhood is culturally specific, archaeological discussion of children's materiality has persistently been influenced by research assumptions which reflect the writers' own understandings of childhood. This has often led to misidentification of material as belonging to children. Most commonly, size or crudeness are taken as evidence that an item was associated with children, through ideas that "since children are…smaller than adults, only children interact with small objects" (Sofaer Derevenski 2000, 7). The usual extension of this is to class such items as toys. Today, children are synonymous with toys (Wilkie 2000, 101), given the afore-mentioned associations of childhood and leisure. This has historically led to assumptions that the same must be true of the past.

The influence of these assumptions is explicit in early reports. Petrie (1890, 30) identified certain wooden items at Lahun as toys called 'tipcats', because they resembled items used in games of his era (Szpakowska 2008, 54). Similarly, at Naqada, he understood a collection of stone blocks and balls in grave 1100 as a bowling game (Petrie and Quibell 1896, 35), although their reconstructed purpose is entirely hypothetical. The excavator's cultural background might also influence what was rejected as children's material. At Deir el-Medina, Bruyère (1939, 102) considered that Bes figurines could not possibly have been appropriate for children, because of their 'erotic' qualities—an outlook grounded entirely in Twentieth Century Western notions of children and sexuality.

The explanation of small items as 'toys', and therefore the preserve of children, is especially prevalent in mortuary contexts. This is true even for items found both with adults and non-adults; "objects in child graves are interpreted in a fundamentally different way to the same artefacts with adults" (Sofaer Derevenski 2000, 6). One example of this is female figurines. Attested in various forms from the Middle Kingdom onwards, these were traditionally interpreted as 'dolls' when with children (Robins 1994, 234-5), and 'concubines' when with adults (Desroches-Noblecourt 1953). The assumption that objects buried with children are toys seems especially frequent with human- or animal-form figurines, which more visually parallel modern playthings. In his excavations of Deir el-Medina, Bruyère (1939, 97) described clay female figurines in graves 1352 and 1375 as toys, as also with a painted flint 'face' in tomb 1159A (Bruyère 1929, 44). He even described grave 1380 as of a "toute jeune fille" (1937, 179) because of the presence of a bread 'doll' with raisins for eyes, although the interred body was 1.72m long!

Despite assumptions based on context and size, such material often has alternative explanations. This suggests that identification of material as belonging to children is usually based on morphology alone (Sofaer Derevenski 2000, 7). To turn to the bread 'doll' from Deir el-Medina, three were found in total (Bruyère 1937, figure 94). The one in grave 1378 was associated with a child's burial, and one from a now-unknown grave apparently also accompanied a child (Bruyère 1937, 106). However, as mentioned, grave 1380 was an adult burial. Being intact and well-preserved, it is unlikely to have originally also contained a child. Such dolls cannot therefore have been only the preserve of children, unless the condition of the individual in 1380 was considered in some way 'child-like'. Possibly they were magic or ritual objects; ritual practice is often open to individualism (Kemp 1995, 26), which might explain their uncommonness. A ritual explanation for the flint 'face' in grave 1159A is also likely. Shaped flints were found in adult graves (Bruyère 1929, 75–6), votive chapels (Bruyère 1934, 69, figure 60), and houses (Bruyère 1939, 270, 276–7, figure 149). Again, that painted and shaped flints were found in a variety of contexts suggests they were not associated solely with children. Occurring in a range of human and animal forms, matching those attested for clay and stone figurines, they may possibly have been rudimentary examples of such votive or protective objects. Certainly, the example from amongst the votive chapels bore a hieratic inscription 'Seth great-of-power, who rages in Heaven at all Gods'.

The expectation that 'toys' will naturally be found in children's graves also assumes that their material corpus reflects the child's own life and experiences. A burial combines physical remains with material signifiers of an individual (Gillespie 2001, 75). However, children's graves represent individuals who have not necessarily built up a lifetime of materially-reflected experience, or passed transitional stages. Burial goods are determined by surviving (adult) kin, and need not reflect the individual as much as the relationships negotiated between living and the dead (Parker Pearson 1982, 112; 1993, 203). Thus, children's burial goods might equally indicate the parents' status, the relationship between parent and child (Pader 1982, 57, 63; Brown 1995, 8), or—in the case of Egypt—wider themes of religion, rather than the children themselves.

Most cases of 'misidentification' cited so far come from the Twentieth Century. There has since been occasional re-evaluation of material previously associated with children. For example, crude clay animal figurines found at Lahun (Petrie 1890, plate 8) and Buhen (Emery et al. 1979, plates 51–4) were traditionally discussed as toys (David 1979). However, rudimentary animals are simple to form, so it is hard to distinguish the work of children from untrained adults (Wileman 2005, 59-60). These objects have been re-considered in recent years; the find contexts of similar examples suggest at least a multivocal use, and many are unlikely to have been associated with children at all (Quirke 1998; Szpakowska 2008, 126). Female figurines have also received re-analysis. Rather than being 'dolls' or 'concubines', they are now believed to have a complex range of ritual meanings related to fertility (Pinch 1983, 1993; Robins 1988; Waraksa 2009; Morris 2011).

However, for the most part, there has been limited recognition of the cultural assumptions upon which scholars based their interpretations. This has two impacts. Firstly, it means that past interpretations are still repeated and persist in modern literature. Despite problems with Bruyère's interpretation of the bread 'dolls' at Deir el-Medina, they are still unquestioningly described as toys eighty years later (for example Meskell 1994, 41; 1999, 173; Booth 2015, 135), as are Petrie's 'tipcats' (Szpakowska 2008: 54). Secondly, it means that cultural assumptions also continue to influence modern analysis. For instance, so-called 'feeding bowls' were found at Lahun and Lisht (Petrie 1890, 20, plate 13). These are generally today assumed to be for feeding infants (Allen 2005, 31), based partly on their size, and partly on their decoration, which bears similarity to that found on 'birthing wands' (Steindorff 1946; Altenmüller 1983, 1986; Quirke 2016). However, in practice, their spouts are too wide to provide a safe flow of liquid for infants (Marshall 2015, 56). Despite their decoration, they are unlikely to have been used for feeding babies. The figures depicted on such items, such as Bes and Tawaret, were not solely associated with children, but also domestic *apotropaia* more generally. Such bowls could equally have been used for feeding the unwell or elderly (Szpakowska 2008, 47).

One problem with children's materiality is therefore incorrectly attributing material to children. The mirror to this is not understanding what should be attributed to them. The misidentification of items as 'toys' reflects misunderstandings about the materials, nature and purposes of play in the past. The idea that children's material inevitably takes the form of toys implies that there is a 'stock' material culture of childhood identifiable in any material record; this ignores the culturally-specific nature of childhood. Indeed, the very assumption that 'toys'—as we would understand them—existed in ancient Egypt is a product of modern Western ideas of childhood as a time of play and social preparation, rather than social contribution. In the modern sense, a 'toy' is a formal category of object, made or purchased by adults for children (Baxter 2005, 42), often in the form of a miniature version of material used by adults. As such, 'toys' frequently incorporate a pedagogical role. They may structure and reinforce social norms, gender roles, or develop physical skills. They are definable in opposition to tools, allowing children to mimic adult actions without real-world consequences (Fortes 1970[1938], 58; Sutton-Smith 1986). In other words, toys impart behaviours in the form of amusement, reflecting cultural separations of work and play, and childhood as a period of preparation and recreation preceding active engagement in social life.

Distinguishing such a category of object in ancient Egypt is misleading. This is not to say that children did not play. It is to say that play was not restricted to its own self-contained sphere of activity, enacted through dedicated material. Art, texts and bioarchaeology all indicate that Egyptian children engaged with work from a young age, as most recently publicised through the discovery of a 'child workforce' at Amarna (Shepperson 2017). Although 'child labour' holds negative associations to a modern Western audience, children were—and often continue to be—vital economic resources (Nieuwenhuys 1996). They did not therefore need to practice and develop skills with 'imitation' objects before enacting them in real life. Discussion of children's materiality, and scope for play, is better served by considering the social contexts within which children were active.

An increasing line of archaeological inquiry involves reconstructing children's introduction to, and participation in, craft activities—for example, pottery production (Kamp et al. 1999; Minar and Crown 2001; Bagwell 2002; Crown 2014). Such studies are grounded in cognitive-developmental frameworks of skills learning (Greenfield and Lave 1982; Lave and Wenger 1991), frameworks which have already successfully been applied to crafts-learning in ancient Egypt (Cooney 2013; Wendrich 2013). It is within such arenas that material traces of children's activities might be recoverable.

Typically, children's initial contributions are useful, but peripheral, at the ends of the *chaîne opératoire*. In pottery production, they might begin by watching the procedure; gathering raw materials; helping to prepare the clay, familiarising them with its material properties; burnishing finished pots; and then gradually adopting responsibility for finished products. Within these arenas, there was scope to combine amusement—experimentation, independence, adult role-play and responsibility—with productive activity. This can even potentially leave material traces. At Deir el-Medina, Bruyère (1933, 16-17) discovered several unrecognisable clay shapes. These were hand-moulded, unfired, and several had small holes or twigs imprinted. He considered them ritual; it is entirely possible that these were formed by children experimenting with the material, possibly in the context of watching or participating in pottery or figurine production. 'Play' was therefore likely enacted within such arenas, through engagements with the same material world as adults.

Alongside work, play potential can be considered in other social activities where children observed and participated, such as household ritual. Children needed to be socialised into religious practice from a young age; much emphasis was placed on the heir as propagator of family cults. The presence of children at ritual activities is suggested textually—O.Cairo 25234 (Daressy 1901: 58, plate 46) references them alongside their parents at a festival dedicated to Amenhotep I—and visually, as the number of mortuary scenes depicting children offering to the deceased alongside adults attest. It is likely that children assisted in domestic rituals. Some archaeological studies have already considered 'play' in the context of children's engagements with figurines, and ritual and religious socialisation (Sillar 1994; Park 1998; Luoti 2007; Kohut 2011), providing a framework for its exploration in Egypt.

A full treatment of these arenas falls beyond the scope of this discussion; it has intended only to suggest directions for future research. The salient point is that children's materiality should not be sought as a discrete sphere, but considered in the context of wider social practices. It is perhaps therefore more accurate to talk of a 'material culture of children' in the past, *i.e.* the materials with which children interacted whatever they might be, rather than a 'material culture of childhood', implying a material world created specifically for them.

Were discussion to end here, however, it would have considered children's activity only in arenas structured by adults. This would be to suggest that children can only be archaeologically 'identified' in relation to adults (Dozier 2016, 61). Discussion of children's materiality must also consider their independent activities, and the material traces these might leave.

It has recently been acknowledged within archaeology that children's peer-structured activities are fruitful for study (Lillehammer 1989, 2000, 2010). Play is not just about escape, but mimicking and practicing skills for use in later life (Hutson 2006, 123). Children do not just passively absorb norms. Peer-activities offer a chance for them to engage with norms imparted through adult-structured activities, on their own terms (Sillar 1994, 49). Children, as future adults, are ultimately responsible for choosing which aspects of culture are maintained or rejected; peer-activities therefore allow children to either reproduce, subvert or reinvent culture (Corsaro and Eder 1990; Corsaro and Molinari 2001, 197). Child-structured interactions can ignore ethnic or rank conventions of adult society, and allow children to create their own social and moral taboos, which can "run counter to formal socialization" (Meckel 1984, 417). Therefore, child-structured play is not completely separate from the adult world. However, it is not dependent on it. Adult-structured activities introduce social values, which children experiment with and adapt on their own terms.

Unlike the materiality of adult-structured activities, which is pre-selected, peer-activities may make use of multiple forms of material. If we try and identify these only with reference to adult perceptions of what constitutes play materials, the child's world becomes inappropriately integrated into that of the adult (Crawford 2009, 62). Archaeologists must instead attempt to access the child's perspective of play. Children can, in theory, interact with anything, but archaeologists are not necessarily programmed to recognise the different perspectives that children have towards material culture (Crawford 2009, 58; for a demonstration of this see Bonnichsen 1973). The materials of child-structured play can perhaps be encapsulated by three types of activities: those using pre-existing materials from the 'adult' world, repurposed by children for their own ends, be that by mimicking adult use or using it in a new way; those using the natural environment, either unmodified or using natural materials transformed via craft or imagination into a new object; and those which involve no physical objects.

Archaeologically, types two and three are hardest to find. Especially when play modified the natural environment, materials would not necessarily survive or be recognised as such. Medieval European sources depict children using household items and the natural environment for play (Crawford 2000, 174; Lewis 2009, 93); without secondary depictions, such activities are inaccessible to archaeologists. However, children's play was not considered suitable for representation in Egyptian formal art. In the few instances where games are depicted (Newberry 1893a, plate 13, 1893b, plates 4, 7, 16, 32; de Garis Davies 1900, plate 21; Blackman 1914, plate 3; Duell 1938, plates 162-5; Simpson 1976, plate 24), a relationship to actual children's activities cannot be assumed. Tomb scenes were always carefully composed, with multiple layers of meaning. These apparently straightforward scenes might instead depict ritual ideas of strength, fertility and vitality, or struggles between order and chaos, represented through children. Indeed, that a limited 'corpus' of games is known, from which all examples draw, strengthens the suggestion that they depict fixed, ritually-invested motifs.

Another line of enquiry is material culture repurposed by children for their own ends. Here, materials might be used in activities replicating their original purpose, or reimagined into something new. Whether or not an object was designed specifically for children to play with, it becomes a plaything as soon as they do (Rossie 2003). In this respect, 'toy' is more of a concept than a material category (Rogersdotter 2008, 143–7). Any object has a potential 'toy-stage' in its use-life (Crawford 2009; Morrison and Crawford 2013), be that alongside its primary use, or as repurposing after it has been discarded. However, it is not enough to say that any object could be used in play. The question is whether this transient 'toy-stage' can be recovered.

One way of identifying potential material is location. Children understand space differently to adults; play activities can transgress cultural conventions for the use of space (Baxter 2005, 63). Theoretically, therefore, items—or concentrations of items—in unexpected find locations could be evidence of their re-use as part of children's activities (Dozier 2016). For example, concentrations of broken faience objects were found dotted around Amarna (Frankfort and Pendlebury 1933, 17). These were interpreted as being too high-quality for the households where they were found; the excavators actually hypothesised that they were collected by children playing near the rubbish dumps. Children were in fact used to explain unusual material locations in certain earlier studies (Bonnichsen 1973; Wilk and Schiffer 1979; Hammond and Hammond 1981; Schiffer 1987). However, in such studies, this material was not used to infer about their lives, nor were investigations explicitly aimed at exploring children. Rather, potential children's distribution patterns were used to better understand adult society (Park 2005, 53–4). Adult behaviour was considered normative; children could only disturb the adult record rather than act as creative forces in their own right, relegating them simply to a site-formation process. Instead, such distribution patterns should be viewed for their potential in understanding children as intentional and independent agents—although children are not the only possible explanation for material movement, especially at sites such as Deir el-Medina or Amarna where much of the material inventory represents abandonment processes.

A second possible criterion is material condition. Objects are more likely to be repurposed by children towards the end of their use in the adult world (Crawford 2009, 63). Archaeologists might overlook these as 'useless' or broken, but even the most unlikely of objects may have been used in play. For example, chipped and rounded pot fragments could have been used as gaming counters. At Lahun, oddly rectangular fragments were found (Quirke 2005, 105), and game boards made of clay or traced on *ostraca* are known (Daressy 1901, plate 31); they were likely also traced ephemerally into the ground. Ad-hoc counters were probably used in these situations. Archaeologists would not automatically assume that a broken sherd has inherent value, but Egyptological studies have shown several uses, such as for winding thread around (Petrie 1917, 53; Cartland 1918). Broken does not automatically mean worthless; current analyses possibly overlook a whole dimension of secondary use and repurposing by children. These avenues require much further consideration.

Children's activities in Egypt therefore enveloped multiple social arenas and levels of participation. However, regardless of arena, because of the conjunction of recreation and other aspects of life, such activities largely incorporate the general material culture of that society, rather than material created specifically for the child. The search for children's materiality is therefore less about specific types of material than it is understanding the social contexts which included children, and how these were materialised.

The problem is that, if a dedicated material world was not created for children, children's materiality largely looks identical to that of adults. If experience is negotiated through materiality, does using what is considered 'adult' material culture make the child's experience that of an adult or child (Sofaer Derevenski 2000, 5)? Indeed, should we even attempt to ascribe the material world of children its own ontological status, or does this itself impose modern distinctions between child and adult?

A further consideration which must be taken into account in future work is that, even if the material world of children is considered as its own ontological category, it is not a homogenised world. Childhood experience varies dependent on class, gender and ethnicity, and all of these factors further inform children's participation in, or prohibition from, social activities. Furthermore, children of different ages, and at different stages of mental and social development, will participate differently in, and in a different number of, social arenas based on their physical capabilities (Fahlander 2008). Without greater knowledge of how childhood was structured and conceptualised in Egypt, these issues cannot be explored, but variation in children's social participation—and therefore materiality—at both the individual scale, and for those of different social conditions, must be expected.

Moving forward

This paper has not exhaustively discussed children's materiality in ancient Egypt. It has aimed to problematise existing research approaches, outline methodological considerations, and suggest avenues for future research. Inevitably, much of the discussion has focussed around 'play'; this is not to say that this is the only activity within which children engaged, but much previous literature has dealt exclusively with this arena, and so inevitably criticism must also. Given children's participation in a range of social arenas, there is plentiful scope for exploration of other aspects of materiality—economic output, costume, and more besides.

Many of the problems discussed in this paper stem simply from the traditional lack of archaeological research into childhood. Childhood archaeology is a relatively new discipline; explicit discussion of children only began in the wake of gender archaeology, in the late 1980s (Diáz-Andreu and Lucy 2005, 7; Baker 1997). Despite having increased in prominence since then, childhood archaeology is still viewed as a niche field, with limited impact on the research methods of wider archaeology (Lillehammer 2010, 16). Archaeologists are therefore not 'trained' to think of children; material is inherently assumed to have been made for and used by adults.

One result of this is that, instinctively, archaeologists often do not think of children as being present at sites unless there are overt reminders of them, such as burials or artistic depictions. Aside from materials misidentified as toys, they are typically 'forgotten' when interpreting the material traces. However, even if a settlement does not present any explicit evidence of children, they were still present, and therefore users—if not producers—of some of the material automatically ascribed to other members of society (Hutson 2006, 105). The difficulty in identifying these traces speaks primarily to problems with current methodologies; shortcomings in the questions asked of material have resulted in a limited ability to discern how children's presence manifests materially. As is often quoted, "children contribute to the archaeological record whether or not we are competent to recognise them" (Chamberlain 1997, 249). A failure to include children in interpretation leads to an incomplete, if not misleading, picture of settlements and their formation processes.

As much as finding new avenues for exploring children's materiality, therefore, a necessary step is to re-evaluate old assumptions. What if, rather than beginning with an assumption that everything belongs to adult contexts, the starting point was that everything relates to children until proven otherwise? Simply 'remembering' children in interpretation—and re-evaluating interpretation in this way—would likely lead to vastly differing conclusions of the same material.

References

Allen, J. P. 2005. **The Art of Medicine in Ancient Egypt**. New York: The Metropolitan Museum of Art.

Altenmüller, H. 1983. Ein Zaubermesser aus Tübingen. **Die Welt des Orients**, 14, 30–45.

Altenmüller, H. 1986. Ein Zaubermesser des mittleren Reiches. **Studien zur Altägyptischen Kultur**, 13, 1–27.

Bagwell, E. 2002. Ceramic Form and Skill. Attempting to Identify Child Producers at Pecos Pueblo, New Mexico. In K. A. Kamp ed. **Children in the Prehistoric Puebloan Southwest**. Salt Lake City: University of Utah Press, 90–107.

Baker, M. 1997. Invisibility as a Symptom of Gender Categories in Archaeology. In J. Moore and E. Scott eds. **Invisible People and Processes: Writing Gender and Childhood into European Archaeology**. London: Leicester University Press, 248–250.

Baxter, J. E. 2005. **The Archaeology of Childhood: Children, Gender and Material Culture**. Walnut Creek: Altamira Press.

Blackman, A. M. 1914. **The Rock Tombs of Meir 1**. London: Egypt Exploration Fund.

Bonnichsen, R. 1973. Millie's Camp: An Experiment in Archaeology. **World Archaeology**, 4(3), 277–291.

Booth, C. 2015. **Lost Voices of the Nile: Everyday Life in Ancient Egypt**. Stroud: Amberley Publishing.

Brown, J. A. 1995. On Mortuary Analysis, with Special Reference to the Saxe–Binford Research Program. In L. A. Beck ed. **Regional Approaches to Mortuary Analysis**. New York: Plenum, 3–26.

Bruyère, B. 1929. **Rapport sur les fouilles de Deir el Médineh (1928)**. Cairo: Institut français d'Archéologie orientale.

Bruyère, B. 1933. **Rapport sur les Fouilles de Deir el Médineh (1930)**. Cairo: Institut français d'Archéologie orientale.

Bruyère, B. 1934. **Rapport sur les Fouilles de Deir el Médineh (1931-1932)**. Cairo: Institut français d'Archéologie orientale.

Bruyère, B. 1937. **Rapport sur les Fouilles de Deir el Médineh (1934-5: II)**. Cairo: Institut français d'Archéologie orientale.

Bruyère, B. 1939. **Rapport sur les Fouilles de Deir el Médineh (1934-1935: III)**. Cairo: Institut français d'Archéologie orientale.

Cartland, B.M. 1918. Balls of Thread Wound on Pieces of Pottery. **Journal of Egyptian Archaeology**, 5(2), 139.

Chamberlain, A. 1997. Commentary: Missing Stages of Life—Towards the Perception of Children in Archaeology. In J. Moore and E. Scott eds. **Invisible People and Processes: Writing Gender and Childhood into European Archaeology**. London: Leicester University Press, 248–250.

Chamberlain, A. 2000. Minor Concerns: A Demographic Perspective on Children in Past Societies. In J. Sofaer Derevenski ed. **Children and Material Culture**. London: Routledge, 206–212.

Cooney, K. M. 2013. Apprenticeship and Figured Ostraca from the Ancient Egyptian Village of Deir el-Medina. In W. Wendrich ed. **Archaeology and Apprenticeship: Body Knowledge, Identity, and Communities of Practice**. Tuscon: University of Arizona Press, 145–170.

Corsaro, W. and Eder, D. 1990. Children's Peer Cultures. **Annual Review of Sociology**, 16, 197–220.

Corsaro, W. and Molinari, L. 2001. Entering and Observing in Children's Worlds: A Reflection on a Longitudinal Ethnography of Early Education in Italy. In A. James and P. Christensen eds. **Conducting Research with Children. Perspectives and Practices**. London: Routledge Falmer, 179–120.

Crawford, S. 2009. The Archaeology of Play Things: Theorising a Toy Stage in the 'Biography' of Objects. **Childhood in the Past**, 2, 56-71.

Crawford, S. and Lewis, C. 2009. Childhood Studies and the Society for the Study of Childhood in the Past. **Childhood in the Past**, 1, 5–16.

Crown, P. L. 2014. The Archaeology of Crafts Learning: Becoming a Potter in the Puebloan Southwest. **Annual Review of Anthropology**, 43, 71–88.

Daressy, G. 1901. **Catalogue général des Antiquités égyptiennes du Musée du Caire**, nos. 25001-25385. Ostraca. Cairo: Institut français d'Archéologie orientale.

David, A. R. 1979. Toys and Games from Kahun in the Manchester Museum Collection. In J. Ruffle, G. A. Gaballa and K. A. Kitchen eds. **Glimpses of Ancient Egypt: Studies in Honour of H. W. Fairman**. Warminster: Aris and Phillips, 12–15.

de Garis Davies, N. 1900. **The Mastaba of Ptahhetep and Akhethetep at Saqqareh**. Part 1. London:

Egypt Exploration Fund.

Desroches Noblecourt, C. 1953. "Concubines du Mort" et Mères de Famille au Moyen Empire. **Bulletin de l'Institut Français d'Archéologie Orientale**, 53, 7–47.

Diáz-Andreu, M. and Lucy, S. 2005. Introduction. In M. Diáz-Andreu, S. Lucy, S. Babić and D.N. Edward eds. **The Archaeology of Identity: Approaches to Gender, Age, Status, Ethnicity and Religion**. London and New York: Routledge, 1–12.

Dozier, C. A. 2016. Finding Children without Toys: The Archaeology of Children at Shabbona Grove, Illinois. **Childhood in the Past**, 9(1), 58–74.

Duell, P. 1938. **The Mastaba of Mereruka**. Vol 2. Chicago: University of Chicago Press.

Emery, W. B., Smith, H. S. and Millard, A. 1979. **The Fortress of Buhen. The Archaeological Report**. London: Egypt Exploration Society.

Eyben, E. 1973. Die Einteilung des menschlichen Lebens im romischen Altertum. **Rheinischen Museum**, 116, 150–190.

Fahlander, F. 2008. Subadult or Subaltern? Children as Serial Categories. In M. Lally and A. Moore eds. **(Re)Thinking the Little Ancestor: New Perspectives on the Archaeology of Infancy and Childhood**. Oxford: Archaeopress, 14–23.

Finlay, N. 1997. Kid Knapping: The Missing Children in Lithic Analysis. In J. Moore and E. Scott eds. **Invisible People and Processes: Writing Gender and Childhood into European Archaeology**. London: Leicester University Press, 203–212.

Fortes, M. 1938. Social and Psychological Aspects of Education in Taleland. **Africa Supplement**, 11(4). Reprinted in: J. Middleton ed. 1970. From **Child to Adult: Studies in the Anthropology of Education**. Austin and London: University of Texas Press, 14–74.

Frankfort, H. and J. D. S. Pendlebury, 1933. **The City of Akhenaten II**. London: Egypt Exploration Society.

Gardiner, A. H. 1937. **Late Egyptian Miscellanies**. Brussels: Fondation Egyptologique Reine Elisabeth.

Greenfield, P. and J. Lave, 1982. Cognitive Aspects of Informal Education. In D. Wagner and H. Stevenson eds. **Cultural Perspectives on Child Development**. San Francisco: Freeman, 181–207.

Gillespie, S. D. 2001. Agency, Personhood, and Mortuary Ritual: A Case Study from the Ancient Maya. **Journal of Anthropological Archaeology**, 20(1), 73–112.

Grimm, L. 2000. Apprentice Flintknapping: Relating Material Culture and Social Practice in the Upper Paleolithic. In J. Sofaer Derevenski ed. **Children and Material Culture**. London: Routledge, 53–71.

Hammond, G. and Hammond, N. 1981. Child's Play: A Distorting Factor in Archaeological Distribution. **American Antiquity**, 46(3), 634–36.

Harlow, M. 2013. Toys, Dolls and the Material Culture of Childhood. In J. E. Grubbs and T. Parkin eds. **The Oxford Handbook of Childhood and Education in the Classical World**. Oxford: Oxford University Press, 322–340.

Hiner, N. R. and J. M. Hawes, 1985. **Growing up in America: Children in Historical Perspective**. Urbana: University of Illinois Press.

Hinson, B. 2017. From the Mouths of Babes: The "*i*-child in Ancient Egypt. **Zeitschrift für Ägyptische Sprache und Altertumskunde**, 144(1), 55-60.

Hutson, S. R. 2006. Children not at Chunchucmil: A Relational Approach to Young Subjects. In T. Arden and S.R. Hutson eds. **The Social Experience of Childhood in Ancient Mesoamerica**. Colorado: University of Colorado Press, 103–131.

James, A. 1998. From the Child's Point of View: Issues in the Social Construction of Childhood. In C. Panter-Brick ed. **Biosocial Perspectives on Children**. Cambridge: Cambridge University Press, 45–65.

James, A. and A. Prout. 1990. **Constructing and Reconstructing Childhood: New Directions in the Sociological Study of Childhood**. Oxford: Routledge.

James, A., C. Jenks and A. Prout. 1998. **Theorizing childhood**. Cambridge: Polity Press.

Joyce, R. A. 2010. Girling the Girl and Boying the Boy: The Production of Adulthood in Ancient Mesoamerica. **World Archaeology**, 31(3), 473–483.

Kamp, K. 2001. Where Have all the Children Gone? The Archaeology of Childhood. **Journal of Archaeological Method and Theory** 8 (1), 1–34.

Kamp, K., N. Timmerman, G. Lind, J. Graybill and I. Natowsky. 1999. Discovering Childhood: Using Fingerprints to Find Children in the Archaeological Record. **American Antiquity**, 64(2), 309–316.

Kemp, B. 1979. Reviewed Work: Commodity Prices from the Ramessid Period. An Economic Study of the Village of Necropolis Workmen at Thebes by Jac. J. Janssen. **Journal of Egyptian Archaeology**, 65, 182–187.

Kemp, B. 1995. How Religious were the Ancient Egyptians? **Cambridge Archaeological Journal**, 5(1), 25–54.

Kemp, B. 2005. **Ancient Egypt: Anatomy of a Civilisation**. 2nd Edition. London: Routledge.

Kohut, B. M. 2011. Buried with Children: Reinterpreting Ancient Maya 'Toys'. **Childhood in the Past**, 4, 146–161.

Koltsida, A. 2007. **Social Aspects of Ancient Egyptian Domestic Architecture**. Oxford: Archaeopress.

Lave, J. and E. Wenger. 1991. **Situated Learning. Legitimate Peripheral Participation**. Cambridge: Cambridge University Press.

Lesko, B. 1994. Ranks, Roles and Rights. In L. Lesko ed. **Pharaoh's Workers: The Villagers of Deir el-Medina**. Ithaca: Cornell University Press, 15–40.

Lewis, C. 2009. Children's Play in the Later Medieval English countryside. **Childhood in the Past**, 2, 86–108.

Lillehammer, G. 1989. A Child is Born: The Child's World in an Archaeological Perspective. **Norwegian Archaeological Review**, 22(2), 89–105.

Lillehammer, G. 2000. The World of Children. In J. Sofaer Derevenski ed. **Children and Material Culture**. London: Routledge, 17–26.

Lillehammer, G. 2010. Archaeology of Childhood. **Complutum**, 21(2), 15–45.

Luoti, K. 2007. Artefacts and Enculturation: Examples of Toy Material from the Medieval Town of Turku. In V. Immonen, M. Lempiainen and U. Rosendahl eds. **Hortus Novus. Fresh Approaches to Medieval Archaeology in Finland**. Saarijärvi: Finnish Society for Medieval Archaeology, 10–20.

Marshall, A. 2015. The Nurture of Children in Ancient Egypt. **Göttinger Miszellen**, 247, 51–61.

Meckel, R. A. 1984. Childhood and the Historians: A Review Essay. **Journal of Family History**, 9, 415–424.

Meskell, L. 1994. Dying Young: The Experience of Death at Deir el-Medina. **Archaeological Review from Cambridge**, 13, 35–45.

Meskell, L. 1999. **Archaeologies of Social Life: Age, Sex, Class et cetera in Ancient Egypt**. Oxford: Blackwell.

Meskell, L. 2000. Cycles of Life and Death: Narrative Homology and Archaeological Realities. **World Archaeology**, 31(3), 423–441.

Minar, C. J. and P. L. Crown. 2001. Learning and Craft Production: An Introduction. **Journal of Anthropological Research**, 57(4), 369-80.

Mizoguchi, K. 2000. The Child as Node of Past, Present and Future. In J. Sofaer Derevenski ed. **Children and Material Culture**. London: Routledge, 141–150.

Morris, E. F. 2011. Paddle Dolls and Performance. **Journal of the American Research Center in Egypt**, 47, 71–103.

Morrison, W. and S. Crawford. 2013. The Archaeology of Play Things: Theorising a Toy Stage in the 'Biography' of Objects. **Childhood in the Past**, 6, 52–65.

Newberry, P. E. 1893a. **Beni Hasan I**. London: Kegan Paul, Trench, Trübner and Co.

Newberry, P. E. 1893b. **Beni Hasan II**. London: Kegan Paul, Trench, Trübner and Co.

Nieuwenhuys, O. 1996. The Paradox of Child Labour and Anthropology. **Annual Review of Anthropology**, 25, 237-51.

Pader, E.-J. 1982. **Symbolism, Social Relations and the Interpretation of Mortuary Remains**. Oxford: Archaeopress.

Park, R. W. 1998. Size Counts: The Miniature Archaeology of Childhood in Inuit societies. **Antiquity**, 72(276), 269-81.

Park, R. W. 2005. Growing up North: Exploring the Archaeology of Childhood in the Thule and Dorset Cultures of Artic Canada. **Archaeological Papers of the American Anthropological Association**, 15, 53-76.

Parker Pearson, M. 1982. Mortuary Practices, Society and Ideology: An Ethnoarchaeological Study. In I. Hodder ed. **Symbolic and Structural Archaeology**. Cambridge: Cambridge University Press, 99–113.

Parker Pearson, M. 1993. The Powerful Dead: Archaeological Relationships between the Living and the Dead. **Cambridge Archaeological Journal**, 3, 203–229.

Parkin, T. 2010. Life Cycle. In M. Harlow and R. Laurence eds. **A Cultural History of Childhood and**

Family in Antiquity. Oxford: Berg, 97–115.

Peck, W. H. 1978. Two Seated Scribes of Dynasty Eighteen. **Journal of Egyptian Archaeology**, 64, 72–75.

Petrie, W. M. F. 1890. **Kahun, Gurob, and Hawara**. London: Kegan Paul, Trench, Trübner and Co.

Petrie, W. M. F. 1917. **Tools and Weapons**. London: British School of Archaeology in Egypt.

Petrie, W. M. F. and Quibell, J.E. 1896. **Naqada and Ballas 1895**. London: Bernard Quaritch.

Pinch, G. 1983. Childbirth and Female Figurines at Deir el-Medina and Amarna. **Orientalia**, 52 (3), 405–414.

Pinch, G. 1993. **Votive Offerings to Hathor**. Oxford: Griffith Institute.

Prout, A. 1999. Childhood Bodies: Construction, Agency and Hybridity. In A. Prout ed. **Body, Childhood and Society**. London: Palgrave MacMillan, 1–18.

Quirke, S. 1998. Figures of Clay: Toys or Ritual Objects? In S. Quirke ed. **Lahun studies**. Reigate: SIA, 145–151.

Quirke, S. 2005. **Lahun: A Town in Egypt 1800 BC, and the History of its Landscape**. London: Golden House Publications.

Quirke, S. 2016. **Birth Tusks: The Armoury of Health in Context – Egypt 1800 BC**. London: Golden House Publications

Robins, G. 1988. Ancient Egyptian Sexuality. **Discussions in Egyptology**, 12, 61-72.

Robins, G. 1994. Review: Growing up in Ancient Egypt. By Rosalind M and Jac. J. Janssen. **Journal of Egyptian Archaeology**, 80, 232-5.

Rogersdotter, E. 2008. **Socializing Children's Toys: An Archaeological Inquiry into Third Millenium BC Harappan Terracotta Remains from Gujarat, India**. Saarbrucken: VDM Verlag Dr. Muller.

Rossie, J.-P. 2003. **Children's Creativity in Toys and Play: Examples from Morocco, the Tunisian Sahara and Peace Education**. Paper delivered at the Fourth Nordic Conference on Children's Play, Hämeenlinna, Finland, 3–6 August 2001. Accessible online at: http://filarkiv.sitrec.kth.se/pub2003/Hameenlinna/textHameenlinna.htm, accessed 07/01/17.

Schiffer, M. B. 1987. **Formation Processes of the Archeological Record**. Tuscon: Maney.

Shepperson, M. 2017. Did Children Build the Ancient Egyptian City of Amarna? **The Guardian**, 6th June 2017. Available online at: https://www.theguardian.com/science/2017/jun/06/did-children-build-the-ancient-egyptian-city-of-armana-, accessed 02/08/17.

Sillar, B. 1994. Playing with God: Cultural Perceptions of Children, Play and Miniatures in the Andes. **Archaeological Review from Cambridge**, 13(2), 47–63.

Simpson, W. K. 1976. **The Mastabas of Qar and Idu. G701 and 702**. Boston: Museum of Fine Arts.

Sofaer Derevenski, J. 1997. Engendering Children, Engendering Archaeology. In J. Moore and E. Scott eds. **Invisible People and Processes: Writing Gender and Childhood into European Archaeology**.

London: Leicester University Press, 192-202.

Sofaer Derevenski, J. 2000. Material Culture Shock: Confronting Expectations in the Material Culture of Children. In J. Sofaer Derevenski ed. **Children and Material Culture**. London: Routledge, 3–16.

Steindorff, G. 1946. The Magical Knives of Ancient Egypt. **Journal of the Walters Art Gallery**, 9, 41-51, 106–107.

Sutton-Smith, B. 1986. **Toys as Culture**. New York: Gardner Press.

Valbelle, D. 1985. Eléments sur la Démographie et le Paysage Urbains d'apres les Papyrus Documentaires d'Époque Pharaonique. **Cahier de Recherches de l'Institut de Papyrologie et d'Égyptologie de Lille**, 7, 75–87.

Waraksa, E. A. 2009. **Female Figurines from the Mut Precinct: Context and Ritual Function**. Freiburg: Academic Press.

Wendrich, W. ed. 2013. **Archaeology and Apprenticeship: Body Knowledge, Identity, and Communities of Practice**. Tuscon: University of Arizona Press.

Wileman, J. 2005. **Hide and Seek: The Archaeology of Childhood**. Stroud: Tempus.

Wilk, R. and M. B. Schiffer. 1979. The Archaeology of Vacant Lots in Tuscon, Arizona. **American Antiquity**, 44(3), 530–536.

Wilkie, L. 2000. Not Merely Child's Play: Creating a Historical Archaeology of Children and Childhood. In J. Sofaer Derevenski ed. **Children and Material Culture**. London: Routledge, 100–113.

Materiality and cultural reproduction in non-elite cemeteries

Rennan Lemos

Introduction

Cultural reproduction has been widely approached on the basis of elite sources and patterns. In general, elite patterns have been interpreted as having trickled down to other social ranks, which assimilated and adapted those patterns. The place and role of non-elite groups in social interactions in ancient Egypt and in other contexts such as Nubia remain unexplored. Examples available only touch briefly upon on the subject, and scholarship has commonly reproduced the idea of a passive reception of cultural patterns by non-elite groups. This is also the case in the context of current discussions of cultural entanglements between Egypt and Nubia. Discussions on the topic tend to emphasise Nubian agency over the acculturation models that until recently dominated Egyptology. However, the role of indigenous non-elites still remains a gap, and a cultural reception approach continues to be adopted in attempting to unveil the place of non-elite groups in social relations.

Here I present some remarks around the idea of cultural reproduction focusing on non-elite mortuary contexts. The arguments summarised here prepare the ground for a 'bottom-up' approach. This approach admits a greater participation of non-elite groups in social interactions, and that this created possibilities for negotiating positions and identities through the active manipulation of material objects often associated with Egyptian elites, which from other perspectives could be viewed as contributing to the reinforcement of existing hierarchies. This paper consists more of a discussion of alternative ways of looking at the available data, than an attempt to provide complete answers to the questions I will address.

The paper begins with a general discussion of cultural reproduction in Egyptology and criticism of elitist, top-down approaches to data deriving from non-elite cemeteries. The paper is anchored in a relational perspective on agency and social hierarchies, emphasising social interactions. A relational view on social hierarchies consists of diminishing the role of 'essentialised' social groups situated in ranks (e.g. 'rich' and 'poor') in favour of examining their interactions with other groups. Therefore, I consider that the materiality of non-elite burials plays an active role in social relationships, making possible the appropriation, re-signification and the subsequent creation of patterns attached to specific contexts of interaction. Examples from New Kingdom non-elite cemeteries are explored in order to preliminarily assess the extent to which these statements find echoes in available data.

Cultural reproduction in ancient Egypt

Today scholarship is extensively aware of the mortuary customs of the elite in ancient Egypt. The subject has been explored since the early days of the discipline, with numerous publications dedicated to different aspects of mortuary customs. Despite this level of knowledge of mortuary customs, the panorama eventually reproduced is a generalised perception of the ancient culture. The study of decorated elite tombs, their objects and texts has served as basis for establishing an outline of the mortuary beliefs and customs of the whole society.

Richards identified this phenomenon as the "tomb problem". In her words, it may be characterised as "a preoccupation with the monumental graves of elite individuals at the expense of accessing the entire range of mortuary behaviour in Egyptian cemeteries" (Richards 2005, 49). Textbooks on Egyptian funerary culture often generalise patterns found in elite contexts as expressing beliefs and practices of the entire population. There are examples that intend to convey variations to the 'rule', though they do not provide an alternative model for interpretation (e.g., Baines and Lacovara 2002). Current scholarship is gradually increasing our awareness of a greater diversity in mortuary behaviour, which includes several strategies of differentiation played by different groups carrying their own ways of conceptualising the world. For instance, Willems recognises that religious knowledge found in elite tombs of the Middle Kingdom correspond to a specific social group (Willems 2014, 214).

Two other phenomena affect the approaches to cultural reproduction in Egyptian archaeology. The first is the discipline's emphasis on textual sources. Overcoming text-aided archaeologies of ancient Egypt still represent a challenge. Egyptian archaeology is still mainly dominated by its focus on textual sources, which may have led to a blurred perception of social diversity, as textual sources express par excellence a specific view on society. In general, material culture provides glimpses from society that are not explicitly present in texts or art (Kemp 1984; cf. Smith 2010, 158–159). Discussions about the limitations of textual evidence are not new in Egyptology (James 1984). Still texts have been widely used in the exploration of social composition and structure in order to unveil the role of different occupations and social groups (Katary 2009).

Scholars agree that from the Middle Kingdom ancient Egyptian literary texts started to mention tangible social events (Parkinson 2002, 13 passim). In this context, new expressions appeared making reference to social groups defined in relation to other groups. For instance, Middle Kingdom texts differentiate 'elite' or 'nobles' from the 'people' or 'lower classes' (Zingarelli 2017, 24). However, owing to the discontinuity between texts and material culture, text-based approaches were revealed to be insufficient to minimize the 'tomb problem', and archaeologies of ancient Egypt have been written grounded upon texts, even though materiality offers its own pathways to interpretation (Wendrich 2010, 276).

The overall problem with a text-based approach is the restrictive representation of the past that comes out. Texts were written and consumed by the smallest elite, and literacy was limited in society. Although various levels of literacy may be identified in ancient Egypt, it is estimated that less than one per cent of the population must have fully dominated the written form of the language (Baines 1983, 584). Exceptions may be seen in workers villages such as Deir el-Medina, which would have been constituted by workers who could write and read. Thus, it makes it difficult to place the village's inhabitants within a specific social rank (Lesko 1994; cf. Ambridge 2007).

Another problem derived from text-based approaches is the fact that the literate elite dominated the possibilities of naming and defining other groups in texts (cf. Zingarelli 2017, 29 passim). This indicates that texts cannot be seen as directly expressing social composition. On the contrary, textual sources express elite strategies of differentiation in relation to other social groups, e.g. the perceptions of the elite on their own place within the social structure, as well as their own view on "minor" and "intermediate" groups.

The Amarna Period offers examples of different levels of literacy. In various erasures of the name of Amun carried out in this period, for instance in the tomb of Amenenhat at Thebes (TT 82), many words carrying the same signs as in the name of Amun were damaged due to misreading and lower literacy levels (Der Manuelian 1999, 288). Archaeology at Amarna also provides examples of appropriation of textual and decorative patterns by non-elite groups in material culture, e.g. 'erroneous' formulaic inscriptions in fragile wooden coffins (Kemp 2012, 262). The non-elites remained outside the context of production of textual formulas and compositions and pictorial patterns, even though these are occasionally found in the materiality of non-elite cemeteries.

Scholars broadly consider the presence of textual formulas in non-elite contexts as emulation of elite patterns by illiterate people. For instance, this is how grammar inaccuracies found in coffins from non-elite burials at Amarna would be interpreted. This view understates agency as it places the non-elites in a passive position within society as a receptacle of elite innovations. Therefore, the elite becomes the driving force of society, spreading in a trickle down fashion its patterns and innovations to other social groups.

A materiality-focused approach may be able to increase complexity in the debate on cultural reproduction. Materiality opens further paths to be explored, including other forms of sociability, and most importantly, non-elite agency. Agency has been a central issue in archaeological theory since at least 1980's; however, scholars have emphasised its vague use throughout the discipline, which has led to some flaws in interpretation (Barrett 2001; Robb 2010).

The discussion on cultural reproduction in non-elite cemeteries may benefit from a 'contextual' understanding of agency. According to Robb, "agency is not a characteristic of individuals, but of relationships; it is the socially reproductive quality of action within social relationships" (Robb 2010, 494). Robb also emphasises the 'relationality' of agency, which materially mediates the entangled relationships between different groups and between them and materiality itself (see Hodder 2012).

This perspective allows us to overcome both the limitations of text-oriented archaeologies of ancient Egypt, as well as approaches lacking consideration of agency to the archaeological record of non-elite cemeteries. The relationality addressed by Robb sheds light onto complex social interactions among which non-elite groups are included. Therefore, the materiality of non-elite cemeteries may be understood as expressing different social interactions between various groups in society. Grounded on this assumption, the debate over cultural reproduction becomes more complex, as emulation and reflection of elite patterns no longer provide complete answers to the questions now proposed to our data sets.

Non-elite manipulations of cultural patterns in materiality now come into focus. It opens space for the recognition of non-elite creativity, social interactions and the strategies of negotiation of positions within different contexts in society through the constitution of social spaces. A relational approach to non-elite agency, in Bourdieu's perspective, would also lead to a breaking "with the tendency to privilege substances—[…] the real groups, whose number, limits, members, etc., one claims to define […] at the expense of *relationships*" (Bourdieu 1985, 723). It thus breaks with the general trend identified in approaches to Egyptian mortuary contexts that aim to recognise, based on objects' quantities and technological characteristics, specific social groups within the materiality of burials (Lemos 2017).

Therefore, I presuppose that we cannot identify specific social groups in the material record, as has been attempted through textual sources. However, following the relational perspective outlined above on agency and cultural reproduction, material culture is considered as part of the network of interactions in which non-elite groups played different roles according to context. Instead of being approached as purely reflecting social inequalities, materiality now becomes pathway of negotiations of positions and identities.

Social interactions replace a trickle-down view of cultural reproduction, as it opens space for non-elite active engagements through materiality. Non-elite engagements consist of contextual negotiations in society through the creation or modification of existent patterns into other ones carrying different meanings and forms. Therefore, cultural reproduction is seen through the lens of social interactions, which express, on one side, non-elite agency and active appropriations of material and cultural patterns, and on the other, the reproduction of existing social hierarchies through the interactions between different groups. Interactions amongst non-elites and other groups produced not only appropriated and re-signified patterns, but also generated new ones after contact with other spaces—both social and cultural.

From trickle-down to relationships: social interactions as cultural reproduction

Veblen's 'The theory of the leisure class' (1899) presented the basis of the trickle-down theory of consumption in neo-classical economics. According to Veblen, new technologies and goods would first be introduced into the market at a price level only affordable by the elites. Then other adapted versions of the same goods would be manufactured as time goes through, making lower classes also able to consume innovations. The trickle-down theory presupposes there is a general tendency in hierarchical societies to spread wealth downwards from higher to lower strata.

Later, Simmel applied the principles of the trickle-down theory to fashion. According to his theory, lower classes would emulate fashion patterns of the higher classes in an attempt to emerge within social structure (Simmel 1904). Although Simmel's theory described some general features of fashion in the beginning of the 20th century, its limits become evident when one considers interactions that produce complex networks of cultural innovations.

Some would agree that the trickle-down theory opens space for the agency of lower classes as it acknowledges their adaptations of elite patterns in order to take part in the social process of consumption. However, this may be considered as just one side of the coin. The trickle-down perspective considers that the elites are par excellence the producers of new cultural trends. The approach does not consider the non-elites as cultural producers while diminishing their own contextual specificities.

A well-established interpretation of cultural reproduction and change in Egyptology is the 'democratisation' perspective. In periods of political decentralisation, cultural patterns previously reserved for royalty passed on to local elites and then to other groups. In the New Kingdom, changes in burial customs in non-elite cemeteries are also interpreted in relation to elite variations in burial assemblages (Goulding 2013; Grajetzki 2003).

The idea of elite emulation has also been applied in other ways in Egyptology. This concerns the idea of Egyptianisation and the interpretation of non-elite mortuary contexts. In the first case, publications conveyed the idea that local lower elites in the Levant adopted the Egyptian style as a reflection of Egyptian control over the area (Higginbotham 2000; Flaminni 2010). Objects from daily life, cultic and mortuary contexts have been quantified and assessed in order to unveil local 'imitations' or 'adaptations' of Egyptian patterns (Mumford 1998). Even when admitting a more complex setting of interactions, conclusions have been drawn based on the perception of an emulation of Egyptian elite patterns. For instance, "burials at Deir el-Balah, Tell el-Farah and Beth Shean have produced locally made Egyptian-derived terracotta anthropoid coffins, local 'grotesque' variants, and sporadic funerary figurines" (Mumford 2014, 78).

In the Nubian case, a perspective of cultural reproduction combined with a notion of Egyptianisation of local populations can also be identified. Models of acculturation of Lower Nubia, though, include a perception of the adoption of Egyptian patterns by local elites as a political strategy in order to gain access to power (Smith 1998). Smith notes that more nuanced interaction-based approaches are adopting resistance, rebellion and ethnic solidarity as analytical foci (Smith 2013, 85).

Recently, Egyptianisation has been widely criticised as an analytical tool. The perspective lacks space for indigenous agency and the capacity for creating their own possibilities through the creative manipulation of material patterns. Egypto-Nubian interactions, for instance, are now seen through the lens of cultural entanglements (van Pelt 2013; Smith and Buzon 2014). The cultural entanglement perspective sheds light onto "the introduction of diversity generated by local choice within the constraints and socioeconomic framework of Egyptian colonial power" (van Pelt 2013, 541).

Even though scholarship has started to highlight indigenous agency, views based on cultural entanglements have focused mainly on the interactions between Egypt and other cultures from an elite standpoint. Appropriations of Egyptian *and* elite patterns by non-elite groups remain understood on the grounds of assimilation (Säve-Söderbergh and Troy 1991). Even when Egyptianisation as a concept has been nuanced or avoided, scholars accept that for non-elite groups "assimilation was top-down, starting with the princes and wealthier members of society and spreading from there to the general population" (Smith 2013, 89).

In both Asiatic and Nubian cases, a lack of local agencies is combined with a trickle-down perception of cultural reproduction. Scholars still see the Egyptian elite as the cultural producer that spreads its patterns on to sub-elites and subsequently to non-elites. The latter hypothetically would adapt outside patterns—both from other cultures and other social hierarchies—into 'grotesque' forms of the same patterns. In order to increase complexity in the discussion of cultural reproduction, we should focus on the relationships and interactions amongst multiple agents considered as producers of culture. Therefore, the trickle down and adaptation/assimilation perspective gives way to a realisation of the active transformations that create and communicate new patterns that serve as material mediators for negotiations of identity and status amid non-elite groups in contexts of social interaction.

In non-elite cemeteries, social structures are reinforced in social interactions at the same time that materiality creates possibilities of negotiating positions through interchanges. Therefore, objects in burials are understood as part of a two-way relationship between interchanges of different groups and cultural reproduction of social structures. From one side, interchanges allow the negotiation of positions and the transit of objects throughout social spaces, while the reproduction of social structures occurs on the basis of the differentiation strategies conveyed in specific cultural settings and patterns materialised in objects.

Social interactions in non-elite cemeteries both allow negotiations to be performed and reinforce existing structures of differentiation. The identification of social interactions is given in the transits of objects across different types of burials attached to different groups. A perspective that emphasises relationships also permits us to realise that people with limited resources were able to create their own material categories in order to negotiate their identity and status.

There is a difference between structural and relational poverty (Mosse 2010, 1157). The former sustains the first. This perspective identifies possibilities of accessing material goods, which makes people able to negotiate their space and identity in context, as well as move throughout different spaces of differentiation. It is people's capacity for crossing social spaces that allows them to negotiate their positions through materiality. However, it is also the movement across spaces of differentiation that reinforces structural hierarchies, as non-elite material creations carry meanings constructed outside elite or sub-elite social spaces. Non-elite agency creates new entangled things after interaction with other groups, allowing them to cross social boundaries. However, those new things reinforce their original place in society, as they do not fit properly outside non-elite social spaces. Therefore, the limits of social fluidity can be seen in the fact that the non-elites can create and materially reshape their world, but cannot effectively be part of other social spaces through which they contextually move.

Social interaction therefore reproduces society and its hierarchies in the creation of new patterns that do examples of how non-elite innovations can reproduce social structures. One may presume that the new pattern found on those coffins does not fit well in the social space within which the black coffin-type was normally used. Differentiations are expressed in the changes of decorative scheme, written inaccuracies etc. But at the same time the coffins convey non-elite possibilities of interacting with social spaces located in a higher social scale, providing non-elite persons the access to cultural patterns that were appropriated in order to create a new entangled object. Entangled objects—a result both of the interactions between different social groups within a given hierarchical structure, and between different cultures—allowed individuals to negotiate their position within individual social spaces, as well as in a broader social setting, creating alternatives that might have worked in specific contexts without changing the main social structure.

Concluding remarks

The examples discussed provide a basis for the perception of the social role of non-elite groups in social interactions. Theirs was an active role, which produced innovations even in a context of domination and colonisation. Considering non-elite individuals as social agents is a way towards overcoming top-down approaches in which a passive role has been attributed to non-elites. However, based on the differences between structural and relational poverty, at the same time that non-elites were able to create their own alternatives, their strategies of establishing social interaction reinforced existing hierarchies. This is due to the fact that their creations would not fit well in other "higher" social contexts.

Therefore, New Kingdom non-elite cemeteries provide a setting where limited material possibilities combine with the power of creating alternatives that open space for other potential interactions. These possibilities include the appropriation of existing material things and cultural patterns, and the creation of new entangled patterns. On the contextual level of relational poverty, alternatives to the norm may arise and play an important role in the constitution of social relations and identities. However, on the level of social structures, non-elite alternatives, identities and worldviews influence little the modification and overcoming of structural poverty and domination/colonisation.

Non-elite agency is expressed mainly in the relational sphere, where they could have access to patterns as they contextually crossed social spaces. Structural poverty, however, remained barely touched. Actually, it was reinforced, as non-elite innovations might have been seen as anomalies within the sets of cultural references shared by wealthier groups.

Acknowledgements

I am grateful to Kate Spence, Paul van Pelt and Fábio Frizzo for discussing the topic with me and for their criticism. Any remaining mistakes are my own.

References

Ambridge, L. 2007. Searching history: the non-elite in ancient Egypt. **History Compass**, 5, 2, 632–645.

Baines, J. 1983. Literacy and ancient Egyptian society. **Man**, 18, 3, 572–599.

Baines, J. and Lacovara, P. 2002. Burial and the dead in ancient Egyptian society: Respect, formalism, neglect. **Journal of Social Archaeology**, 2, 5, 5–36.

Barrett, J. 2001. Agency, the duality of structure, and the problem of the archaeological record. In I.

Hodder ed. **Archaeological theory today**. Cambridge: Polity, 141–164.

Binder, M. 2014. Preparing for eternity. In N. Spencer, A. Stevens and M. Binder. **Amara West: living in Egyptian Nubia**. London: British Museum Press, 69–84.

Bourdieu, P. 1985. Social spaces and the genesis of groups. **Theory and Society**, 14, 6, 723–744.

Brunton, G. and R. Engelbach. 1927. **Gurob**. British School of Archaeology in Egypt.

Der Manuelian, P. 1999. Semi-literacy in ancient Egypt: some examples from the Amarna Period. In E. Teeter and J. A. Larson eds. **Gold of Praise. Studies on Ancient Egypt in Honor of Edward F. Wente**. Chicago: Oriental Institute, 285–98.

Flammini, R. 2010. Elite emulation and patronage relationships in the Middle Bronze Age: the Egyptianized dynasty of Biblos. **Tell Aviv**, 37, 154–168.

Giorgini, M. S. 1951. **Soleb II. Les nécropoles**. Firenze: Sansone.

Goulding, E. 2013. **What did the poor take with them? An investigation into ancient Egyptian Eighteenth and Nineteenth Dynasty grave assemblages of the non-elite from Qau, Badari, Matmar and Gurob**. London: Golden House Publications.

Grajetzki, W. 2003. **Burial customs in ancient Egypt: life in death for the rich and poor**. London: Duckworth.

Higginbotham, C. 2000. **Egyptianization and elite emulation in Ramesside Palestine: governance and accommodation on imperial periphery**. Leiden: Brill.

Hodder, I. 2012. **Entangled: an archaeology of the relationships between humans and things**. Oxford: Willey and Sons.

James, T. G. H. 1984. **Pharaoh's people: scenes from daily life in imperial Egypt**. London: Tauris Parke.

Katary, S. 2009. Distinguishing subclasses in New Kingdom society on evidence of the Wilbour Papyrus. In J. C. Moreno García ed. **Élites et pouvoir en Égypte ancienne. Cahiers de Recherches de l'Institut de Papyrologie et d'Égyptologie de Lille**, 28, 263–319.

Kemp, B. J. 1984. In the shadow of texts: archaeology in Egypt. **Archaeological Review from Cambridge**, 3, 2, 19–28.

Kemp, B. J. 2012. **The city of Akhenaten and Nefertiti: Amarna and its people**. Cairo: American not find place in elite social spaces. This makes us able to acknowledge both non-elite agency and the structural limits imposed on those groups.

Glimpses from non-elite cemeteries

Social interactions as cultural reproduction have twofold meanings. Firstly, it happens in the active appropriation, access and use of outside patterns (both culturally and from other social spaces). Those patterns are converted into new entangled material objects carrying other meanings. Secondly, it is perceived in the invention of new contextually exclusive patterns.

Objects typically associated with elite mortuary contexts are occasionally found in non-elite contexts. However, usually those objects vary in shape, appearance, use and materials. Variations were commonly conveyed as poorer adaptations or copies of elite patterns, although they may be seen today as expressing non-elite agency, creativity and the capacity to provide themselves with other cultural patterns that would allow them to cross boundaries amongst social spaces. This is the case, for instance, with stelae found at the South Tombs Cemetery of Amarna. The majority of the excavated examples are undecorated and not as smoothly carved, though some of those who lived under the same conditions were able provide themselves with more elaborated and inscribed ones (Kemp et al 2013, 69).

At the New Kingdom colonial city of Amara West in Nubia archaeologists have found the fragments of a female coffin lid in tomb G309. The fragile fragments depict a red-skinned face wearing a black wig. In the Egyptian tradition, it is uncommon to find red-painted faces in female coffins from the period (Binder 2014, 77). This coffin may be an example of the use of available patterns in a new fashion. For instance, the coffin seems not to carry any inscriptions—usually found in Egyptian examples—and the red face could have been translated into another pattern in local ground. It may consist of a creative innovation conveying the interaction between cultures and social hierarchies in an entangled object.

When found in non-elite burials, objects containing texts may be considered the most emblematic example of social interactions. In the same way that non-elite-made objects were interpreted as less sophisticated adaptations, the materiality of non-elite texts has been considered the clearest example of non-elite copies. As discussed before, the levels of literacy in ancient Egyptian and Nubian societies must have varied considerably within different social spaces. Even though non-elite groups were able to provide themselves with textual objects, their command of the written language must have been insufficient or null. This is indicated by grammatical inaccuracies found in inscribed objects in non-elite contexts. However, instead of classifying non-elite textual objects as simple adaptations or copies of richer models, those objects show us again non-elite agencies operating at contextual levels. This demonstrates the possibilities for non-elite groups to interact with other groups in order to have access to alternative cultural patterns and subsequently to produce culture by themselves in new entangled patterns.

The New Kingdom cemetery at Medinet el-Ghurob provides us with various examples of inscribed objects found in non-elite burials. Some of those objects were inscribed for people who occupied official positions within the administration of the harem-town, e.g. the shabtis of Menkheper, mayor of Medinet el-Ghurab under Ramses II (Brunton and Engalbach 1927, 11). Such objects do not necessarily indicate they were used in the burials of those individuals whose names we read in inscriptions. Inscribed objects from Medinet el-Ghurab burials may express the possibilities of lower groups to access elite patterns and objects in order to give those objects new meanings and material functions in context. This is also the case of a canopic jar lid found in one of the largest shaft tombs. In the cemetery, there are no traces of mummification, so one should question the function of a canopic jar in such a context. Though as the site was widely looted, this proposition remains a hypothesis, which requires verification against examples provided by other cemeteries.

In New Kingdom cemeteries in Nubia, a pattern found in larger shaft tombs is their collective use. Unlike elite tombs in the Theban necropolis, which were intended for a single wealthy individual, in cemeteries like Fadrus (tomb 511), Soleb (tomb 11) and Qustul (tomb V48), a great number of individuals was found in larger tombs (Säve-Söderbergh and Troy 1991, 219; Giorgini 1971, 159; Williams 1992, 272). Those tombs provide examples of refined objects such as stelae, masks and inscribed wooden anthropoid coffins. To what extent those tombs represent wealthier individuals or local elites or sub-elites remains a question to be further explored. However, one may assume as a possibility that community engagement would increase non-elites' possibilities of interacting with other groups, therefore being more effectively able to negotiate their identity and position within the social hierarchy (see Stevenson 2009).

Social interactions as both setting for innovation and agency, and also cultural reproduction can be realised in the different material patterns and uses of appropriated objects in non-elite contexts. On the coffin fragments inscribed with the name of Senisenbu at Qustul for instance, the name of Osiris has been incorrectly written, with the throne being substituted by the *rs* sign, as well as the *n* sign (Williams 1992, 153). As with the red-faced coffin found at Amara West, the anthropoid coffin of Senisenbu found alongside non-elite burials probably represents a real individual who created a new pattern for inscribing the name of Osiris.

At the South Tombs Cemetery at Amarna, archaeologists found a set of anthropoid wooden coffins, some decorated with figures of humans and gods and formulaic inscriptions (Kemp et al 2013, 71). The coffins were mainly made of sycamore and tamarisk wood, with gypsum and lime plaster, materials which can be found locally (Skinner in Kemp 2015, 29). Those coffins are comparable with examples found elsewhere in Egypt and Nubia, especially at Qustul and Fadrus. Intersection of social spaces and social fluidity are mainly recognised in inscriptions on the coffins. The texts were reproduced inaccurately on the coffins' surfaces, also attesting access to and other uses of cultural patterns existing within higher social spaces. However, the non-elite coffins at Amarna also provide the identities of some of the individuals buried within, alongside their titles. The most remarkable example is the coffin of Maya, lady of the house, whose mask was carved in an exquisite way (Kemp and Stevens 2008; Dolling 2008; Bettum in Kemp 2015). Although the Amarna coffins were usually restrained in terms of their materials, signs of golden leaf were found in the burials (Bettum in Kemp 2015, 31), which is comparable with anthropoid coffin masks from non-elite burials at Fadrus. The rare realgar pigment was also attested in some of the Amarna coffins (Skinner in Kemp 2015, 29), which comprises one more element for the realisation of non-elite agency and movement across social spaces in order to provide themselves with materials that would make negotiations of identity and positions more effective. A similar case is a female individual found in a pit burial at Fadrus carrying on her hands a blue faience scarab inscribed for the 'God's wife, Meryt-Amun' (burial 147) (Säve-Söderbergh and Troy 1991, 261). It is also an example of use and appropriation of available cultural patterns in local context with the aim of negotiating power and establishing differentiation.

The Amarna non-elite coffins comprise the most remarkable example of social interactions and non-elite agency available as they attest more than the creative appropriation of cultural patterns materialised in new entangled objects. The coffins exemplify the creation of a new, non-elite specific coffin type, created through social interactions and interchanges. According to Bettum, "the Amarna coffins with ritual scenes [comprise] a special sub-type of the black anthropoid coffin used in the Eighteenth Dynasty" (Bettum in Kemp 2015, 32).

Although the coffins from Amarna may be considered a new, *non-elite* coffin type, they are also

University in Cairo Press.

Kemp, B. J. 2015. Tell el-Amarna, 2014-15. **Journal of Egyptian Archaeology**, 101, 1–35.

Lemos, R. 2017. Material culture and social interactions in New Kingdom non-elite cemeteries. In J. Chyla, J. Dębowska-Ludwin, K. Rosińska-Balik and C. Walsh eds. **Current Research in Egyptology 2016. Proceedings of the Seventeenth Annual Symposium**. Oxford: Oxbow, 121–135.

Lesko, B. 1994. Ranks, roles and rights. In L. Lesko ed., **Pharaoh's workers: the villagers of Deir el-Medina**. Ithaca: Cornell University Press, 15–39.

Mosse, D. 2010. A relational approach to durable poverty, inequality and power. **Journal of Development Studies**, 46, 1156–1178.

Mumford, G. 2014. Egypt and the Levant. In A. E. Killebrew and M. Stein eds. **The Oxford Handbook of the Archaeology of the Levant c. 8000–332 BCE**. Oxford: Oxford University Press, 69–89.

Richards, J. 2005. **Society and death in ancient Egypt: mortuary landscapes of the Middle Kingdom**. Cambridge: Cambridge University Press.

Parkinson, R. 2002. **Poetry and culture in Middle Kingdom Egypt: a dark side to perfection**. London: Continuum.

Robb, J. 2010. Beyond agency. **World Archaeology**, 42, 4, 493–520.

Säve-Söderbergh, T. and L. Troy. 1991. **New Kingdom Pharaonic Sites: the Finds and the Sites**. Partille: Paul Åström.

Simmel, G. 1904. Fashion. **The American Journal of Sociology**, 62, 6, 541–558.

Smith, S. T. 1998. Nubia and Egypt: interaction, acculturation and secondary state formation from the Third to First Millennium BC. In J. Cusick ed. **Studies in culture contact: interaction, culture change, and archaeology**. Carbondale: Illinois University, 256–287.

Smith, S. T. 2010. A portion of life solidified: understanding ancient Egypt through the integration of archaeology and history. **Journal of Egyptian History**, 3, 1, 155–185.

Smith, S. T. 2013. Revenge of the Kushites: assimilation and resistance in Egypt's New Kingdom empire and Nubian ascendancy over Egypt. In G. Areshian ed. **Empires and complexity: on the crossroads of archaeology**. Los Angeles: Cotsen Institute of Archaeology, 84–107.

Smith, S. T. and M. Buzon. 2014. Colonial entanglements: "Egyptianization" in Egypt's Nubia empire and the Nubia dynasty. In D. Welsby and J. Anderson eds. **The Fourth Cataract and beyond. Proceedings of the 12th International Conference for Nubian Studies**. Leuven: Peeters, 431–442.

van Pelt, W. P. 2013. Revisiting Egypto-Nubian relations in New Kingdom Lower Nubia: from Egyptianization to cultural entanglement. **Cambridge Archaeological Journal**, 23, 3, 523–50.

Veblen, T. 1899. **The theory of the leisure class: an economic study of institutions**. New York: Macmillan.

Wendrich, W. 2010. Epilogue. Eternal Egypt deconstructed. In W. Wendrich ed. **Egyptian archaeology**. Oxford: Blackwell, 274–278.

Willems, H. 2014. **Historical and archaeological aspects of Egyptian funerary culture. Religious ideas and ritual practice in Middle Kingdom elite cemeteries**. Leiden: Brill.

Williams, B. 1992. **Excavations between Abu Simbel and the Sudan frontier: New Kingdom remains from cemeteries R, V, S and W at Qustual and Cemetery K at Adindan**. Chicago: Oriental Institute.

Zingarelli, A. P. 2017. Introducción. La literatura egípcia antigua: una aproximación al pensamiento y a la sociedad. In A. Zingarelli y V. Mayocchi eds. **Relatos del antiguo Egipto**. Buenos Aires: Biblos, 13–34.

The sap of life: materiality and sex in the divine birth legend of Hatshepsut and Amenhotep III

Uroš Matić

"Our translations of words like *nfr* are deplorably flat and lacking in the sap of life"

Adriaan de Buck (after Gardiner 1950, 52).

Introduction

Many anthropologists and archaeologists insist that materiality is more than simply matter or material culture. Scholars also consider that the study of materiality should deal with the understanding of dynamic relations between subjects and objects, people and things (Fahlander 2008, 129; Joyce 2015, 181, 184; Meskell 2005, 6–7; Miller 2005, 4; Tilley 2007, 17). The main problem is that, in the meanwhile, materiality became a theoretical buzzword (Ingold 2007, 2; Knappett 2014, 4701). Sometimes even entire works are titled 'materiality of-' although the term itself and its usage are never defined explicitly, but have to be indirectly understood by the reader as social interpretation of sensory experience of material world (e.g Tilley 2004). Discussions on materiality in ancient Egypt are indeed rare and tend to focus on, for example, the biography and agency of objects and phenomenological approaches to landscape (Meskell 2004; Rummel 2016).

The notion of materiality as 'socialness of things' (Fahlander 2012, 140; Tilley 2007) strongly resembles now several decades-old discussions on the difference between sex and gender and if such a difference exists at all. Before the third feminist wave and queer critique, sex was understood both in anthropology and archaeology as a biological division of male and female bodies different in chromosomes, sex organs, hormones and other physical features. Gender was understood as the socio-cultural interpretation of these differences (Matić 2016, 810–811). The division between sex and gender was criticised by queer theorists and was argued to be a consequence of heteronormativity (Butler 1990, 1993). Sex does not exist without social meanings, and the way in which we understand gender is essentially the way we understand sex, because materiality is bound up with signification from the start (Butler 1993, 30). The premise of third-wave feminism and queer theory that bodies matter, that sex is always already gender and that it is being fixed, naturalised and materialised through performative citations of established gender norms (Butler 1990, 1993) also found its way in archaeology (Perry and Joyce 2001). However, if one understands materiality as socialness of things and transfers this to the sex/gender division debate, there is a danger of understanding gender as 'socialness of sex' which is exactly not the point of the queer view of materiality. Judith Butler actually argued for 'matter, not as site or surface, but as a process of materialization that stabilizes over time to produce the effect of boundary, fixity and surface we call matter' (1993, 9). Although she primarily discussed this in the context of materialisation of sexual difference, Butler's ideas are valuable for theorizing other bodily differences too. Nevertheless, her concept of materiality was also argued to be limited because it focuses exclusively on human bodies and social factors (Barad 2007, 34). For Karen Barad, matter is a dynamic and shifting entanglement of relations and not just a property of things (2007, 35). Materiality therefore goes beyond the properties of things in themselves and implies the attribution of other properties through entanglement. We should take into account body's anatomy and physiology and other material forces including those nonhuman ones (Barad 2007, 65). Following Barad, we should explore the relations between humans and non-humans and how the entanglements of these relations come to produce different materialities. In fact the question is not only if people in other geographical or temporal contexts sensed surfaces, textures, smells, and tastes, and felt pleasure, pain, and sorrow, differently or as we do, but also what evidence do we need in order to know that (Hamilakis 2013, 6). Feminists and queer theorists are not at ease when talking about bodies and materialities as things made of flesh. This is because they insist that, by assuming the flesh behind them, it is often forgotten that the physiology of bodies is formed in the domain of the discourse. Therefore they ask the questions what flesh, where and when? And which discourse, when and where? (Povinelli 2006, 8). It seems that the main problem with representationalist accounts on materiality as 'socialness of things' is the assumption that discourse and matter are separated instead of mutually constituting and interdetermining (Marshall and Alberti 2014, 26–28). Egyptology is in a good position to deal with this nuanced theoretical discussion because it benefits from the existence of both textual, iconographic and archaeological sources in broader sense. It can, as a discipline, benefit from drawing inspiration from current discussions in archaeology just as much it can contribute to these discussions.

Following the previously outlined concept of materiality and the recent archaeological focus on sensory aspects of the past, this paper deals with the material, tactile and sensory aspects of the divine birth legend of the king. In the narrative, the queen mother encounters the divine father of her child. From an anthropological and archaeological perspective to materiality, I aim to bring back substance and a sensorial aspect to this ancient Egyptian text. Also, such an approach allow us to discover new matter-realities, or new assemblages of matter, as one attributes properties to matter which are not inherent to the things themselves, opening space for other materialities and bodies.

The main sources analysed in this paper are written and visual attestations of the divine birth legends of Hatshepsut and Amenhotep III from Deir el-Bahari and Luxor temples. The paper also touches upon the problem of the translation of the ancient Egyptian lexeme *nfr* in the texts of the divine birth legends of Hatshepsut and Amenhotep III. It is proposed that phallus, one of the well-attested meanings of the lexeme *nfr*, is possibly alluded to in the text describing the erotic encounter and indeed sexual intercourse between the queen and the god Amun. This suggestion was already made by other authors who did not follow it further and did not provide arguments to support it (DuQuesne 2005, 9, 13; Rikala 2008, 117).

Bringing matter back to the text of the divine birth legends of Hatshepsut and Amenhotep III and considering all the sensory aspects of the event described in it is crucial for the apprehension of the idea behind the text. This idea is the ontogenesis of the ruler in his divine nature. All of the material and substantial aspects of the text are related to the divine phallus and what it produces, namely the sap of life—the divine seed and eventually the divine ruler. The discussion in this paper therefore leads to the discussion on materiality and divine substance as a plea for an ontological turn (Viveiros de Castro 2015; cf. Graeber 2015) in anthropological and archaeological theory, and potentially in Egyptology. It is suggested that anthropologists and archaeologists should explore other *matter-realities* if they want to better understand other worlds and bodily differences in them, both past and present. In the words of Judith Butler, by unsettling 'matter' as we understand it, one opens new possibilities and ways for bodies to matter (Butler 1993, 3). Archaeologists working with the ideas of Karen Barad and Eduardo Viveiros de Castro stress the importance of materials without being deterministic, as well as question the humanocentrism of our interpretations of the past (Marshall and Alberti 2014, 20). Such an approach is also advocated in this paper.

Divine birth legends of Hatshepsut and Amenhotep III

Ancient Egyptians conceptualised their kings as sons of gods at least since the Old Kingdom. That the king was the son of Re is explicit in his epithet *s3 Rˁ* 'son of Re'. We are also informed from Papyrus Westcar (Papyrus Berlin 3033, 9. 9–10) about certain Ruddjedet described in the following way (Blackman 1988, 11–12):

ḥm.t wˁb pw n(j) Rˁ nb-S3ḫb.w jwr.tj m ḫrd.w 3 n(j) Rˁ nb-S3ḫb.w

'She is the wife of a wab-priest of Re, Lord of Sakhebu, she being pregnant with 3 children of Re, Lord of Sakhnebu'.

It is interesting that the wife of the priest of god Re is the one carrying the children of the god. These children are later in the text described in divine terms. Ruddjedet is attended in delivery by goddesses Isis, Nephthys, Meskhenet and Heqet, goddesses associated with birthing and Khnum, the creator of humankind. It is worth mentioning that almost all of these deities are part of the later texts and the iconographic program of the divine birth legend of Hatshepsut and Amenhotep III. These deities are also associated with re-birth and eternal life (Taterka 2017b, 264). Reference to them is only one of many connections between the story from Papyrus Westcar and the later divine birth legends of Hatshepsut and Amenhotep III.

Although ancient Egyptian sources inform us that the king is the son of god there is really no consensus among Egyptologists on the nature of the king in ancient Egypt. Some Egyptologists took a stand that it was the institution, not the one who held it as a position, that was considered to be divine (Grimal 1986; Goedicke 1960; Posener 1960). Thus, Georges Posener argued that the king's qualities and capacities are different and inferior to those of the gods (1960). However, the king's human traits can be also found among the gods, which lead others to argue that the divinity of the king had to be achieved, as he was not divine from his very birth (Hornung 1982, 142). Joachim Friedrich Quack argued that even the individual kings were considered to be different than human and emphasised that this is clearly an ontological issue and that it can be hardly resolved (2010, 1). Without an attempt to resolve this complex question, in this paper I advocate for the position that ontological differences matter and that one should not aprioristically consider neither semblance nor difference when bodies of human and divinities are concerned. These bodies should be re-constructed in the analysis. Egyptologists have often interpreted ancient Egyptian narratives on the nature of the king, such as the divine birth legend, as propaganda (e.g. Myśliwiec 2004, 84). Others have criticised the use of this term. If we understand propaganda as information of biased and misleading nature used to promote mass control, then this term is not adequate considering the audience in question, the access to the texts, their visibility and the background knowledge of those who were able to read them (Baines 1994, 81, 85; Vernus 1995, 164). Luc Gabolde rightfully reminded that if the audience was divine the notion of propaganda as false reality fails, because one cannot lie to a god (2014, 33).

It is clear that the divine birth legend dates back much earlier than the examples from the reigns of Hatshepsut and Amenhotep III studied more closely in this paper. This is indicated both by the Second Intermediate Period Papyrus Westcar, as mentioned above, and by the earlier divine birth legend scenes from the central lane of the causeway of Senwosret III at Dahshur with a speech of Re and references to divine birth of Senwosret III (Oppenheim 2011, 171, 183). To these one can now add a fragment of the scene of circumcision from the pyramid complex of Djedkare (excavation number 426) which has parallels in later Middle and New Kingdom scenes of circumcision within the divine birth legend cycle (Megahed and Vymazalová 2015, 275–277). One should also mention the rarely-mentioned relief blocks of Senwosret I from Elephantine reconstructed by Werner Kaiser as part of the barque sanctuary (figure 1). Here we find the king Senwosret I and goddess Satet depicted in a similar way as queen Ahmose and god Amun are depicted in the divine birth scenes of Hatshepsut in Deir el Bahari (figure 2) or queen

Mutemwiya and god Amun are depicted in the divine birth scenes of Amenhotep III in Luxor.

Figure 1. Block with a relief depicting Senwosret I with goddess Satet, Elephantine, reconstructed by Werner Kaiser as part of the barque sanctuary, photo by Uroš Matić.

One has to consider the depiction of Senwosret I and goddess Satet in the context of his textual and iconographic royal program, which served as an inspiration for Hatshepsut (Iwaszczuk 2014). Therefore, various fragments of the divine birth legend are attested in text and image since the Old Kingdom, which makes its appearance during the reign of Hatshepsut and Amenhotep III less unique than previously thought. The divine father during the Old and Middle Kingdom is Re, as indicated both in the reliefs from Dahshur and in Papyrus Westcar, whereas this role during the New Kingdom is played by Amun, although there are attestations of Senwosret I mentioning that he is the son of Amun (Gabolde 2014, 33). One interesting exception would be the case of Senwosret I possibly being the divine father/partner with Satet as his divine consort. This remains to be investigated further.

But how do we explain the divine birth legend in terms of ontology? In my opinion, the entire notion of propaganda and uniqueness in the case of Hatshepsut at least, stuck to the text of her divine birth among scholars so long because of the supposed exceptionality of her rule as a female king. The entire idea of propaganda in the case of the divine birth legend of Hatshepsut must be related to the consequent *queering* of her rule by scholars (e.g. Breasted 1908, 77). Yet, she was not deceiving anyone, and it is naive to think that her subjects did not know she was a woman (Matić 2016). She also does not differ from previous rulers by referring to her divine birth. Clearly, focusing solely on ideological aspects of the divine birth legend does not do justice to the general idea behind it, the divine ontogenesis of the king.

Figure 2. Ahmose and Amun, Third Scene, Middle Colonnade, Northern Wall, Deir el-Bahari (after Naville 1897: Pl. XLVII).

The texts of the divine birth legend of Hatshepsut and Amenhotep III do not differ significantly in composition. Both of the texts narrate that a mortal woman who happened to be either queen Ahmose, mother of Hatshepsut, or Mutemwiya, mother of Amenhotep III, attracted the attention of the god Amun. The god himself addresses other gods and says that he loved the queen loved by the king (Urk. IV, 216. 10–217.17). Amun then consults with the god Thoth on how to approach her. He states that he met her in Karnak. Thoth then tells him that she is more beautiful than other women in the entire land and that she is the wife of the king. He then leads Amun, who took the form of the king, to the queen (Urk. IV, 219). What happens next is well known to Egyptologists, yet they tend to keep one eye shut on the fact that in order for Hatshepsut and Amenhotep III to be conceived, Ahmose and Mutemwiya had to have sex with god Amun. I am not implying that Egyptologists are blind on the fact of this sexual intercourse, my point is rather that they usually do not go into the details of this erotic encounter, although there are some very welcomed exceptions to this (Frandsen 1997, 84–93; Quack 2017, 33–34; von Lieven 2013, 159). Some Egyptologists used the term 'sacred marriage' to describe the union of the god and the queen (Assmann 1982, 16; DuQuesne 2005, 10) and thus, although implying sexual intercourse, distanced themselves from comments on the details of this very same intercourse. That god Amun also had pleasure, sexual, reproductive or recreational, is rarely acknowledged (Harvey 2003, 88). Egyptologists are stressing 'the risk of over interpretation and vulgar simplification' (Frandsen 1997, 84) or are 'discretely leaving the couple at this point of the story' (von Lieven 2016, 309). However, if we are to discuss bodies, substances and fragrances, and thus other *matter-realities*, as suggested above, sometimes we have no other option than to invade privacies. Indeed, as historians and archaeologists, scholars of the people in the past, this is all we ever do. Studying the details of this encounter by concentrating on its material and sensory aspects can not only enrich our understanding of the text itself but also allow us to re-think some other related texts and consequently think anew the divine body in ancient Egypt.

It is interesting to remark that both women approached by Amun, namely Ahmose and Mutemwiya, are married as is Ruddjedet mentioned in Papyrus Westcar. One could say that the Egyptian gods prefer married women. Some authors suggest that a 'sacred marriage' between the queen and the god was important for legitimising royal succession, referring to Ahmose as god's wife of Amun (DuQuesne 2005, 10). However, one has to bear in mind that Ahmose is not attested with this title yet and that there is actually no evidence that Mutemwiya also bore the title (Gitton 1984, 61, 93). Thus, although not being 'god's wives of Amun' they were visited by the god and the details of this encounter will be analysed next.

The meaning of *nfr* in texts describing the divine conception of Hatshepsut and Amenhotep III

The text of the divine birth legend continues stating that the god in the form of the king found the queen in her palace. The part of the text which is of our interest here states (Urk. IV. 219, 13–220.6):

gmj.n=sn n sndm=s m nfr.w nw ꜥḥ=s	'They (the king and the god) found her resting in the *nfr.w*-chamber of her palace.
(s)rs.n=s ḥr stj nṯr	She woke up because of the god's scent.
sbṯ=s ḫft ḥm=f	She smiled in view (lit. in the face) of His Majesty,
sw šmj=f ḥr=s ḥr-ꜥ	and then he went to her immediately
sw ḥꜣd=f r=s	and he spread out to her,
sw rdj(=f) jb=f r=s	and gave his heart to her,
sw rdj(=f) mꜣꜣ=s sw jm=f n nṯr	and let her see him in his form of a god,
m-ḫt wj=f tp-jm=s	after he previously came to her.
ḥꜥj.tj m mꜣꜣ nfr.w=f	This one (queen) rejoiced in seeing his *nfr.w*.
mrw.t=f hpj=s m ḥꜥ.w=s	His love went into her body.
ꜥḥ bꜥḥj m stj nṯr	The palace was flooded with the god's scent,
ḫnm.w=f nb.w m Pwnn.t	all of his smells are from Punt.'

This part of the text is rich in erotic motifs. It is interesting that it opens in plural form. Namely, the king and the god embodied in him found the queen in the palace. But then the text refers to the god's scent in singular after which the queen smiled in view of His Majesty again in singular. This indicates that being asleep she could not see the incoming figure but only smell him and she smelled a god. But after waking up because of god's scent she saw her husband. He then went to her, spread out to hear and gave his heart to her and let her see him (His Majesty) in his divine form after he already came to her previously as His Majesty. This is how the god reveals himself and ends the possible confusion. After letting her see himself in the god's form she rejoiced in seeing the god's *nfr.w*. His (the god's) love went into her body and the palace was flooded with the god's scent from Punt. God's scent, queen's smile, king's/god's spreading towards her, the entering of his 'love' into her body, the flooding of the palace with the smells of Punt, all strongly indicate sexual intercourse. An interesting question is what is this *nfr.w* the queen rejoiced in seeing?

The semantic field of the word *nfr* in ancient Egyptian is vast ranging from 'to be good' and 'to be beautiful' to 'to be complete, perfect' and 'to be completed, accomplished, finished' (Wb 2, 253.1–

256.15; 257.7; cf. Stock 1951). Like many other Egyptian words it does not have a single equivalent in English language. The lexeme *nfr.w* is most often translated as beauty, although it could also mean sunshine, precious things, offerings, good things and well-being (Wb 2, 260.1–11). This verbal noun is clearly constructed by the edition of the ending *–w* on the verbal root *nfr*. Adriaan de Buck suggested that the notion of young, new, triumphant life was inherent in this word (Gardiner 1950, 52). According to Hanns Stock basic meaning of the root *nfr* is a state of maturity or ripeness as much as an end or completion (1951, 5–8). Giulio Farina and Thomas Schneider relates it to Arabic *nabula* 'to be precious, noble, refined' (Farina 1924, 324; Schneider 1997, 1999). Considering sound correspondence close similarity is found in Bedawiye (Bedja) *nāfir* 'sweet, pleasant, comfortable' (Takács 1999, 369). This might be one of the reasons why this word was chosen to sometimes signify the phallus of a god next to all other associations such as completeness, beauty and perfection for example. In the context of the divine birth legend most of the authors indeed translate this verbal noun as 'beauty' (Breasted 1908, 80; Helck 1961, 225; Reineke 1984, 102; Myśliwiec 2004, 84), 'radiant vitality' (Frandsen 1997, 84), 'splendor' (Barbotin 2004, 10), 'completeness' (Brunner 1986, 43) or 'perfection' (Coyette 2015, 91). They however do not explicitly state how they understood the role of this word in the passage quoted above which leads us to conclude that they assumed the most widely accepted understanding of this lexeme when translating the passage.

There are several other texts where *nfr* unequivocally signifies the phallus of a god (cf. Blackman and Fairman 1950, 71; Walker 1996, 271). This is clear both from the context and from the orthography of the word, namely the use of phallus determinative. Such a meaning of the lexeme *nfr* is not surprising considering the suggested basic meaning of maturity or ripeness (Stock 1951, 5). Thus, in the Papyrus Anastasi III (Papyrus British Museum 10246 Rto, line 5,1) it is said about a statue of god Thoth that 'his *nfr* is of carnelian' *nfr=f n ḥrs.t* (Gardiner 1937, 25). The lexeme *nfr* is here written with a phallus determinative. One only has to look at the colour of this stone to understand why it was used for this body part. The colour of the stone and the colour of the glans of a phallus are strikingly similar so that one can indeed speak of transference of material properties from a stone to the flesh and vice versa. This is especially clear if one thinks about the statue of Thoth in the baboon form considering the colour of baboon's penis in erection. The hymn to Thoth in Papyrus Anastasi III does indeed refer to him as a baboon radiant of mane-*wbḫ mḥw.t* (Gardiner 1937, 25). In the Papyrus Sallier IV (18, 3–4) of the 19th dynasty Isis is attested as seeing Min's *nfr* (Münster 1968, 130). The lexeme *nfr* is here written without a phallus determinative. Inscription in the hall of the Amun temple at El Hiba with the hymn of Darius I or Darius II to Amun is even more explicit as it describes Amun as 'the husband which shoots with his phallus' *hȝy stj.w nfr.w=f* (Brugsch 1878, Tf. XXVI, col. 27). Here, not only is the lexeme *nfr.w* written with a phallus determinative but the meaning of the lexeme in this context is indicated by the verb *stj* which among else has the meaning 'to shoot semen out' as also indicated by the use of the phallus determinative in such cases (Wb 4, 329). Thus, it is clear that the *nfr.w* he is shooting with is actually his penis. In the Ptolemaic inscriptions from the Edfu temple (Edfu I, 398. 10-11) the goddesses rejoice in seeing the *nfr* of Min (Wilson 1997, 515). This is a phrase we have already seen in the text of the divine birth legend, namely *ḥʿj.tj m mȝȝ nfr.w=f* 'This one (queen) rejoiced in seeing his *nfr.w*'. We have also realised that seeing of Min's *nfr* by goddess Isis is also attested in 19th dynasty Papyrus Sallier IV. That the same word, in our case *nfr/nfr.w*, can have different meanings should be neither new nor surprising. One should only think about various words used for phallus in English language which on the first glance have nothing to do with this word (e.g. cock, bird, prick, willy, wiener). In Latin the words for sharp and pointed instruments (penetrative) are used to signify a penis, such as *virga*-'branch, rod' or *caraculum* 'stake' or *gladius* sword, among many (Adams 1982, 14–21).

Indeed, metaphorical language in New Kingdom Egyptian love poems was already recognised as 'concealment of eroticism' and it was argued that there was a deliberate concealment of explicit language and the use of words for 'obscene' and sexual conducts (Hsu 2014, 407). Some authors relate this to religious decorum arguing that explicit sexual intercourse was not depicted because it is incidental and inappropriate for temple context (Frandsen 1997, 89). Similarly, divine birth of Hatshepsut is also described as 'one of the most serene and chaste representations of sexual intercourse ever devised by men' (Dorman 2014, 5). The attestations in which the lexeme *nfr/nfr.w* means phallus are indeed, although not much, later than the text of divine birth legend of Hatshepsut. However, this is not the reason enough not to consider the additional meaning of this lexeme in this particular context, at least not when considering all the evidence at hand. In fact when used to designate a phallus, the word *nfr* designates the phallus of a god and is as such also attested in temple contexts written with a phallus determinative. The phallus determinative is indeed lacking in the writing of the verbal noun *nfr.w* in the texts of the divine birth legend, but does this mean that eroticism is therefore concealed? The use of different language to express erotic connotations does not necessarily mean the lack or concealment of eroticism. Indeed, the phallus determinative was written in the word *ḥ³d* 'to spread out' (Wb 3, 36.10). This leads us to conclude that if they wanted the scribes could have written the word *nfr.w* in the divine birth legend text with a phallus determinative. They obviously choose not to do this. One possible reason for this is that by not writing the phallus determinative they preserved the ambiguity of the passage. This ambiguity was already strengthened by the reference to the king and the god in plural and interchangeable references to the king and the god in one body. It is the divine phallus which is refered to as *nfr/nfr.w* in ancient Egyptian texts and in this particular context we are dealing with both the king and the god in one.

It is our modern pornographic gaze which often stops us from recognising erotic elements in those places where they are not as explicit as we need them to be in order to recognise them. At the same time this 'pornographic gaze' can be put to use in bringing back substance and erotic details in understanding the text describing the sexual encounter between the queen and Amun. There are other indications that the overall context is erotic and that the queen rejoiced upon seeing god's phallus even if we do not translate the lexeme *nfr* here solely as phallus. Namely, after she was awaken by his scent, the queen smiled at him and it is then that he went to her instantly and the text then uses the verb *ḥ³d* 'to spread out' written with a phallus determinative. Paul J. Frandsen understands this verb in this passage as 'having an erection towards' (1997, 84) which is indeed indicated both by the meaning of the verb 'to spread' and therefore 'to erect' and the phallus determinative. Similarly Alexandra von Lieven suggested 'in Erreugung geraten'-'to be arroused' (2013, 159). New Kingdom Egyptian love songs similarly use verbs such as *kf³* 'to open' (Wb 5, 121.1) to indicate sexual intercourse, like in pChester Beatty I C 3,1 (Hsu 2014, 408). The next line *rdj(=f) jb=f r=s* 'he gave his heart to her' is also one of the ways to refer to actual sexual intercourse (Frandsen 1997, 86). After she rejoiced at seeing his *nfr.w*, 'his love' (*mrw.t=f*) came into her body (limbs), and only then was the palace flooded with god's scent coming from Punt. We know that ancient Egyptian gods take pleasure in smelling the scent of aromatic gums and resins and incense has the power to transform space into one suitable for divine presence (Harvey 2003, 83). But we also know that the word *mrw.t* can also allude to sexual intercourse in New Kingdom Egyptian love poems (Hsu 2014, 409). Additionally, in love/erotic poetry of the New

Kingdom Egypt scents are associated with an erotic atmosphere, so that the scent of flowers or plant essence radiates from the body of the beloved person (Hsu 2014, 411; Verbovsek and Backes 2015, 109–110). In one case we also find a parallel situation to the one described in the divine birth legend. In the text preserved on the Ostracon Deir el-Medina 1266+Ostracon CGC 25218 (15-16), the arms of the female lover are spread out to a male lover like something from Punt when he hugs her and she smells like misy-flowers, which smell like labdanum (Verbovsek and Backes 2015, 110). The scent of love entering her body and the origin of that scent are crucial for our understanding of the materialisation of that love (*mrw.t*). Thus, whether or not phallus of the god Amun was implied behind the word *nfr.w* in this particular context does not change the fact that the god had to have an erection in order to have intercourse with the queen and that he indeed had it, as implied among else with the use of the verb *ḥꜣd*. The consequence being that even if the phallus of the god is maybe not meant most directly, nevertheless it is an erect penis which constitutes his *nfr.w* the queen rejoiced seeing. This is only one of the senses used by the queen in this erotic encounter. The second important sense worth discussing in all of its material aspects is smell.

There are two lexemes, which are used for the aromatic plants originating from Punt *ꜥntj* and *snṯr*. Their translations as myrrh and frankincense are conventions and different scholars suggest different identifications of these plants, thus for *ꜥntj*-*Pistacia terebinthus*, *Gummi arabicum* and *Acacia Senegal* (for a summary of arguments see Breyer 2016, 107–119). Thus, as Francis Breyer showed in his most recently published study on Punt, these aromatic plants are still puzzling as neither the lexemes, nor the representations can help us in identifying them with certainty and the distribution of different aromatic plants from both sides of the Red Sea also does not narrow the choices down (Breyer 2016, 107–119). One thing is however clear, whether or not behind these lexemes stands one plant or the other, their products were used as aromatic scents in temple rituals. Not many plants in the regions variously interpreted as the location of the land Punt (south-east Africa or west Arabian Peninsula) have the property to produce this specific aromatic resin. The ones that do are harvested in a specific way. Frankincense resin begins first as a milky-white sticky liquid that flows from the trunk of the scrubby tree Boswellia when it is injured, healing the wound. Frankincense resin flows when a tool (nowadays called a *mengaff* or *sonke*) is used to scrape about a five-inch section down the trunk of tree (Espinel 2017, 25). Frankincense is used by the Jordanian population nowadays even as an aphrodisiac and fertility promotion agent, with this property being scientifically tested and confirmed, at least on rats (Nusier, Bataineh, Bataineh and Daradka 2007, 365–369). However, one has to bear in mind that the incense associated to gods in ancient Egypt comes from cultic burning of already hardened incense resin. The sensory experience associated to incense is primarily the smell of burned incense and not the smell of fresh sap coming from an incense tree. Nevertheless, fresh resins are often fragrant enough so that we can safely assume that, although there was clearly a sensory difference between the fresh and the hardened burned resins, these states of the incense emanated the same note of scent. Egyptians were familiar with the qualities of the fresh resin considering the fact that incense trees were transported to Egypt already during the Old Kingdom. There are depictions of the king Sneferu, founder of the 4th dynasty inspecting trees brought from foreign lands on the scene from his so-called Valley Temple in Dahshur. Trees brought from Punt are also depicted in the mortuary temple of Sahure of the 5th dynasty from Abusir (Taterka 2016, 117). On two reliefs (SC/south/2003/07 and 06) from this temple there is a depiction of the extraction of resin from *ꜥndw* trees with the use of *ꜥnt* adze. The resin is yellowish brown (El-Awady 2009, 155–186, pls. 5–7). The incense trees from Punt are among the products loaded on Egyptian ships and brought from the expedition to Punt as evidenced by reliefs from Deir el-Bahari (Naville 1898, Pls. LXIX and LXXIV). They were planted in the garden of Amun (Naville 1898, Pl. LXXVIII). In the foreigners' procession scene from the tomb of Rekhmire (TT 100) from the reign of

Thutmose III there is a register with Puntites bringing *jn.w* among which is an incense tree looking the same as the trees depicted on Deir el-Bahari reliefs (Hallmann 2006, 37–38). Therefore, the properties of resin in all of its states was well known to the Egyptians.

An analogical relation between resin and sperm presents itself as quite plausible in the context of the description of the body of a god and its sensual effects. Such analogies were not strange to ancient Egyptians. One only has to think about the episode of the Contending of Horus and Seth in which Isis placed the sperm of Horus on the lettuce eaten by Seth, as attested in Papyrus Chester Beaty I (recto 11,1–13,5) from the reign of Ramesses V, or on in a temple inscription from Edfu (I, 82.5–6; II, 44.12–13) from the Ptolemaic period in which the lettuce plant and its semen are offered to Min in order to defeat his enemies. This lettuce was argued to be associated with sperm because of the milky sap when cut (Schukraft 2007, 307–313). It is the colour, which relates the sap of the lettuce with sperm in this case, and it is both colour and stickiness as a quality of substance which relate sperm and frankincense liquid. Thus, as white sticky liquid pours from the tree, which produced frankincense, so does pre-seminal fluid or sperm pour out of the phallus of Amun in erection and during ejaculation. One should remember that the text states 'This one rejoiced in seeing his *nfr.w*. His love went into her body' (*ḥʿj.tj m mȝȝ nfr.w=f mrw.t=f ḥpj=s m ḥʿ.w=s*). As argued above, whether or not phallus was explicitly meant behind the lexeme *nfr* here, the fact is that the god had an erection and an orgasm. Liquid from the incense tree is the sap of life which fertilises the queen and eventually leads to the birth of the new divine ruler. In the divine birth legend scene the god is depicted giving life to the queen in the form of an *ʿnḫ* sign which he brings to her lips with his left hand and places on her palm with his right hand (Fig. 2). This gift of life is his love (Frandsen 1997, 86). The process of emergence of mineral, oily, and oleoresinous products would be associated in priestly discourse to important divine episodes (Aufrère 2017, 4). The divine birth legend texts of Hatshepsut and Amenhotep III are indeed one of such divine episodes.

Divine substance

The result of the union of god Amun with the queen are the births of Hatshepsut and Amenhotep III. I have argued above that crucial for the understanding of the texts of the divine birth legend, at least when the union is concerned, are the substances and their physical aspects (colour, smell, texture etc.). These are also crucial for both divine and human bodies and this is exactly where we once again observe ontological differences. As noticed by Stephen P. Harvey the scent of Amun forms a textual link between the divine birth legend and the Punt scenes. Both narrate on the bringing of the divine substance to Thebes. In the case of the divine birth legend through impregnation of the queen with the divine seed and in the case of Punt expedition through bringing incense to Egypt (Harvey 2003, 89). I have argued above that there are strong arguments suggesting that the seed of Amun and the liquid of the incense trees were considered to be related in their materiality. They share the material physical properties such as colour and consistency. However, we should not confuse ourselves easily and suggest that ancient Egyptians could have perceived sperm smelling like frankincense, but we can suppose that they thought the sperm of Amun smells like that. This is because the human and the divine body are different in nature but probably similar in culture (*sensu* Viveiros de Castro 2015).

Not surprisingly, Hatshepsut's body, born of a human mother and conceived by the divine father Amun, has all of these divine characteristics. In an inscription accompanying the scene of offering of the products brought back from Punt to Amun-Re it is stated that the king (Hatshepsut) measured the heaps of offerings and that Hatshepsut herself was acting with her arms. The same text also contains the description of her body (Urk. IV, 339.13–340.2):

ḥm.t=s ḏs=s jr.t m ʿ.wj=s *ḥȝ.t ʿnt.w ḥr ʿ.wt=s nb.(w)t* *ḫnm.w=s m jd.t nṯr* *jw stj=s ȝbḫ(.w) m Pwn.t jnm=s nbj(.w) m ḏʿm* *ḥr-ʿbȝ mj jr.t sbȝ.w m ḫnw* *wsḫ.t ḫft ḥr n tȝ r ḏr=f*	"Her Majesty Herself gives with her both hands the best myrrh upon all her limbs. Her fragrance is that of a god, her scent mingling with that of Punt, her skin is gold-platted with electrum, with glittering visage like the stars do (appear) in the interior of the festival hall in the presence of the entire land."

Hatshepsut herself put myrrh upon her limbs and mingled her own scent with that of Punt in order to emphasise her own divine nature as the female counterpart of Amun. The causal connection between Amun's engendering of Hatshepsut and qualities of her body is not explicitly made in the text presented here. Clearly, in practice Hatshepsut had to anoint herself or be anointed in order to smell of products of Punt, but the text describes the qualities of her body. The same is the case of Thutmose I or Thutmose IV approaching their queens Ahmose and Mutemwiya. These men had to put ointments smelling of Punt on themselves in order to smell like Punt, however, maybe in thinking like this we miss one point. The placement of myrrh on her limbs is clearly related to the ritual actions undertaken by the female king but it is also related to her divine ontogenesis.

Already Erik Hornung argued that the scents of Punt brought by Hatshepsut and the glittering gold are central for her divine-ness (Hornung 1982, 64, 134). As Christophe Barbotin also noticed, the ruler is divinised by the gold and scents of Punt coming from the divine union between the god Amun and the queen (2004, 11). As it is well known, Amun is attested as a deity from Punt and protector of this land (Urk. IV, 345. 6–8). We should also bear in mind, that one of the reasons Punt was designated as the 'god's land' is its geographical position in relation to Egypt as it lay in the south-east, the direction in which the sun and other celestial bodies rise (Cooper 2011: 49; von Lieven 2016, 310). In the Edfu temple inscriptions of the Ptolemaic period Punt is attested as the birthplace of the sun god (Breyer 2016, 425). Later in antiquity we are informed from the Theophrastus' account of the Sabaeans in which he states that the sun is the patron of both frankincense and myrrh, but also cinnamon (Detienne 1994, 7). This later and culturally distant account is nevertheless important because it directly states what is hinted by the ancient Egyptian sources, namely the association of sun and frankincense. It is not surprising that the qualities of substances and materials can be fused as in the case of Hatshepsut's skin being fashioned from electrum and glittering, like the stars (celestial bodies) in the interior of the festival hall, but at the same time emitting the aroma of Punt. It is the sun itself and the scent itself of both the god (Amun-Re) and this god's land (Punt), which are embodied both in the frankincense and in Hatshepsut. Her body is literally made out of these substances, which have qualities we would maybe not ascribe to them. Namely, that electrum of her skin smells like aromatic plants from Punt is a consequence of the fact that the body of her father is made of gold and his semen is like the substance from these plants. This is specific for New Kingdom Egyptian notions of materiality, which does not have to coincide with ours or any other's. As Alexandra von Lieven pointed out the connection to the gods in ancient Egypt cannot be restricted solely to the so called sacred animals, as often argued, but it transcends into the realm of animals and plants, celestial bodies and minerals, the entire inhabited and uninhabited nature filled with the divine (2004). Utte Rummel similarly demonstrated that the appearing of goddess Hathor is directly associated with the materiality of the Theban cliffs, material metaphor of the body of Hathor-Imentet (2016, 51–55).

In the case of Hatshepsut we are seeing the creation of the female king's body, a 'material ontogenesis' of her divine body from the semen of Amun, which is the white sticky liquid of the frankincense trees.

Her glittering body with the skin of electrum reminds of the dried out white liquid turned into yellowish-brownish glittering frankincense. We should remember that properties of materials are in flux (Ingold 2007; Tilley 2007, 17). Just as the products of the trees from Punt are in flux, from white liquid to shiny, glittering and sunny and star like chunks, so is the body of the king going through the same 'phylogenesis'. It therefore does not surprise that Amun's daughter is associated to the same land and its substances, because she is herself literally originating from his own body. If one compares the chunks of frankincense with chunks of gold ore or simply with chunks of gold one can notice a close similarity. It is probably not a mistake to bring stars into this equation too. The texts do not indeed make a direct connection to the engendering of the female king through Amun and the description of her body, so that one can say that the description of her body is a consequence of Punt expedition. However, her engendering through her divine father Amun is what later brings her to organise the expedition to Punt.

The aroma of the female king Hatshepsut mingling with that of Punt and her skin gold-platted with electrum and having glittering visage like the stars are also allusions to goddess Hathor. Thus, as some archaeologists insists, working with the ideas of Karen Barad referred to in the paper's introduction, we should take seriously the assertion of a material equivalence between very different kinds of bodies (Marshall and Alberti 2014, 20). The identification of Hatshepsut with goddess Hathor in the context of Punt scenes and accompanying texts was already emphasised by Filip Taterka (2016, 116; 2017a, 44). Here I will follow this emphasis further and provide supportive arguments based on the description of Hatshepsut's body and its associations to some attributes of goddess Hathor. The goddess Hathor is in the text of Hathepsut's Punt expedition attested as the 'mistress of Punt' and 'mistress of incense' (Urk. IV, 323, 5; Urk. IV, 324, 1). She is also well attested as associated to gold and stars. Gold and gold dust are often associated to Hathor and she is also known as the golden one (Finnestad 1997, 213). According to Hornung gold as the flesh of gods is attested from the Middle Kingdom onward (1982, 134) Additionally, one should stress that gold and electrum are prominent among the goods brought back from Punt expeditions or delivered by the Puntites and are referred to as coming from the land of Amu which is associated with Punt (Meeks 2003, 65). Hathor is attested as the mistress of stars $nb.t\ sb^3.w$ already in the Story of Sinuhe (Allen 2015, 143).

It is also worth mentioning that although later, Hathor of Dendera is called 'daughter of Re' and in Philae she is known as 'the female Horus' ($Ḥr.t$), assuming many solar aspects of these two gods (Finnestad 1997, 213; Inconnu-Bocquillon 2001, 197–198). She is known as the female falcon $bjk.t$ (Leitz et al. 2002, 77). According to an inscription from Edfu temple the female falcon is also associated to oleoresins as their production results from emotion. Oleoresin ^3ḥm manifests itself in the uterus of the female falcon after her heart complained while crossing the land of Punt. Bearing this mytheme in mind the connection with Hathor and the Puntite scenes from Deir el-Bahari were already made (Aufrère 2017, 7). One should also mention that in the Punt inscriptions Hatshepsut is, at the same time, Amun's daughter and his female counterpart (Urk. IV, 332, 10–14). Different aspects of her divine nature are stressed in different context. Her role as the divine daughter is clearly stressed in her divine birth scenes whereas her role as $R^ʿ.t$ or possibly Hathor in the Punt scenes. These natures are not mutually exclusive. Maybe the first place to look for the parallel for a body made of precious metals and smelling of incense would be the cultic revelation of the divine statue. At the same time, considering the idea that ancient Egyptian gods could indwell cult statues (Meskell 2004, 89–92), one should consider the possibility that Hathor in the context of the above quoted description of Hatshepsut's body indwells the body of the queen just as she would indwell a statue of herself. One can even go so far and say that Hathor can be born as a queen just as she can be born as a statue, with both the queen's body and the statue of the goddess being Hathor's twt 'image' (cf. Kjølby 2009, 36–37). This is what Lynn Meskell termed 'distributed notion of the divine self' (2004, 90). Taking this into consideration the semblance of the queen's body with the body of a goddess or her statue is not surprising. Indeed, a statue does not emanate incense but is rather offered with incense, just as the body of the queen is anointed with myrrh and does not emanate myrrh. However, this brings us to the question raised by archaeologists advocating the so called ontological turn: what is left of representationalism when the represented becomes present (Marshall and Alberti 2014, 21)? Whichever way certain effects are achieved they are still there and there semblance to other bodies with the same effects cannot be denied. The semblance of the bodies of the queen and the goddess, possibly even her statue, can be summarised with the idea that if the king is understood as the image of a god, then the image of the god must be the same as king's image, which does not lead to the loss of identity (Bayer 2014, 15). We have seen this in the episode of the divine birth legend in which the king and the god are referred to in plural 'they (the king and the god) found her resting in the *nfr.w*-chamber of her palace'. The queen mother (Ahmose or Mutemwiya) then interacts with both of them interchangeably. According to Hornung the statues of gods were made of precious materials so that they can resemble the flesh of gods and thus allow them to enter the statues (Hornung 1982, 135). In the same way the body of Hathsepsut has to be like the statue and the body of Hathor in order for the goddess to be embodied in her.

The divine nature of Hatshepsut is also reflected in the text on the southern wall of the southern middle portico of the temple in Deir el-Bahari which states that a seated statue of Amun and a granite statue of herself were sent to the land of Punt. The same text which mentions these statues identifies her as both the god's majesty and his daughter (Taterka 2016, 116). The Puntites received the statues of a god and a goddess. One is even tempted to consider the ancient Egyptian divine birth legend and its connection with Punt and its aromatic products as an inspiration for later myths and legends such as the above mentioned female falcon crossing the land of Punt or the Greek legend of Myrrha, also known as Smyrna. She is the mother of Adonis and she was transformed into a myrrh tree after tricking her father Cinyras to have sexual intercourse with her. Myrrha gave birth to Adonis while she was in the form of a tree (Detienne 1994, 2). It would be erroneous to identify Hatshepsut with Myrrha and Amun as her father Cinyras, however it is interesting that certain elements, although in different constellation do appear in both legends. It was also suggested that the roots of all these myths and legends is a Somali myth about the queen who lost her kingdom and her children and who receives compensation from the god in the form of frankincense and myrrh trees which grew where her tears would have run (Aufrère 2017, 7).

Conclusion

Returning substance and material properties to the ancient Egyptian texts and the events they describe brings us closer to their social background. This allows us to understand the nuances of ancient Egyptian lexemes and their usage better and to give substance to those nonhuman actants usually left out from the action. By bringing back matter to the text of the divine birth legend I argued that the lexeme *nfr*, as used in the episode of Amun's encounter with queens Ahmose and Mutemwiya, is to be understood not only with its general meaning 'beauty' but also with its additional sense as the phallus of the god Amun, as also attested in later texts which explicitly refer to the divine phallus. The main arguments I presented for this interpretation are:

1. Overall erotic context of its usage in the episode of Amun's sexual union with queens Ahmose and Mutemwiya.

2. Later parallel attestations of its usage to signify the phallus of a god (Amun, Min, Thoth) as evidenced both by the orthography (phallus determinative) and the context-although the phallus determinative is not written in the divine birth legend texts.

3. Material properties of the scent of Amun originating from Punt and identified as frankincense or myrrh which is first and foremost a white sticky liquid and only after drying a glittering mass of brownish lumps. Only after *mrw.t* (love and semen) of Amun entered the body of the queen did the entire palace smell like Punt. The semen of Amun is like the god himself related to the land of Punt. His semen relates to Punt through its materiality which gives it properties of incense tree and the sun. The god himself relates to Punt through his Puntite origin.

4. Description of Hatshepsut's body in which all of the material properties of the body of her divine father are merged (scent of Punt, glittering skin made of electrum). At the same time these attributes are the attributes of Hathor who is known both as the mistress of Punt and mistress of incense and as the golden one. In the Punt inscriptions Hatshepsut is referred to as $R^c.t$ or female Sun. All of this indicates that she has both the divine nature being Amun's daughter and taking the role of Amun-Re's counterpart in Punt scenes. These roles are complementary so that her body is equally divine because of her origin and because of her actions.

This coming together of things such as plant products (incense), metals (gold), flesh (skin) and fluid (sperm), usually separated in conventional categories, is encompassed by theoretical notions of networks and assemblages. These are understood as open-ended and heterogeneous collections of entities and as such they allow things to come into existence as a consequence of their relations (Marshall and Alberti 2014, 20). That a skin of electrum smells like frankincense is something with which Egyptologists probably find hard to reconcile. Yet, these substances have to be in a specific assemblage in order to be experienced in this way. We have to acknowledge that materials in ancient Egypt were not classified according to the same nomenclature as today and the tension emerges when one classifies materials on 'objective' criteria-real world or from a mythological point of view-divine world (Aufrère 2017, 2). Difference of materials should be produced in the analytical process and not assumed before the analysis (Marshall and Alberti 2014, 23). *Matter-realities* are thus different assemblages, which produce different experiences of substances. We do not recognise other matter-realities because we do not share the same assemblages. In the words of Karen Barad we lack the appropriate apparatus (Barad 2007, 145–146). The assemblage in question, namely sun-gold-frankincense-divine seed, is characteristic for god Amun and parts of this assemblage are characteristic for his daughter Hatshepsut and his divine consort Hathor. In line with the ontological turn in anthropology (Viveiros de Castro 2015), Egyptology has to enrich the world of ancient Egypt with agencies of various entities. This must be done even when the choice of partner in sexual intercourse is concerned. Only when we include both human and non-human in writing accounts on bodies based on ancient Egyptian texts will we have the appropriate apparatus to understand specific ancient Egyptian notions on matter and the body better than we do now.

Acknowledgments

I would like to thank the editors for inviting me to contribute to this volume. I am grateful to Dietrich Raue for pointing me to the relief of Senwosret I from the reconstructed barque shrine at Elephantine. I also thank to Rune Nyord and Filip Taterka for providing me with some of the references, reading the draft thoroughly and making useful comments and insights which both helped me to improve my arguments and challenge my ideas. My acknowledgements for useful comments and references also go to Alexandra von Lieven, Joachim Friedrich Quack, Julia Hamilton, Roxana Flammini and Danijela Stefanović.

Bibliograhy

Adams, J. N. 1982. **The Latin Sexual Vocabulary**. London: Duckworth.

Allen, J. P. 2015. **Middle Egyptian Literature. Eight Literary Works of the Middle Kingdom**. Cambridge: Cambridge University Press.

Assmann, J. 1982. Die Zeugung des Sohnes. Bild, Spiel, Erzählunh und das Problem des ägyptischen Mythos. In J. Assmann, W. Burkert, F. Stolz eds. **Funktionen und Leistungen des Mythos. Drei altorientalische Beispiele**. Orbis Biblicus et Orientalis 48. Fribourg und Göttingen: Universitätsverlag, 13–61.

Aufrère, S. 2017. Egyptian myths and trade of perfumes and spices from Punt and Africa. In I. Incordino and P. P. Creasman eds. **Flora Trade Between Egypt and Africa in Antiquity**. Oxford: Oxbow, 1–16.

Baines, J. 1994. On the Status and Purposes of Ancient Egyptian Art. **Cambridge Archaeological Journal**, 4. 1, 67–94.

Barad, K. 2007. **Meeting the Universe Halfway: Quantum Physics and the Entanglement of Matter and Meaning**. Durham and London: Duke University Pres.

Barbotin, Ch. 2004. Pount et le mythe de la naissance divine à Deir el-Bahari. **Cahiers de Recherches de l´Institut de Papyrologie et d´Égyptologie de Lille**, 24, 9–14.

Bayer, C. 2014. **Die den Herrn Beider Länder mit ihrer Schönheit erfreut-Teje. Eine ikonographische Studie**. Ruhpolding: Verlag Franz Philipp Rutzen.

Blackman, A. M. and H. W. Fairman. 1950. The significance oft he ceremony Hwt bHsw in the temple of Horus at Edfu. **Journal of Egyptian Archaeology** 36: 63–81.

Blackman, A. M. 1988. **The Story of King Kheops and the Magicians. Transcribed from Papyrus Westcar (Berlin Papyrus 3033)**. Reading: J. V. Books.

Breasted, J. H. 2008. **Ancient Records of Egypt.** Vol. 2. The Eighteenth Dynasty. Chicago: University of Chicago Press.

Breyer, F. 2016. **Punt. Die Suche nach dem »Gottesland«**. Leiden and Boston: Brill.

Brugsch, H. 1878. **Reise nach der grossen Oase el Khargeh in der lybischen Wüste**. Leipzig: J. C. Hinrichssche Buchhandlung.

Brunner, H. 1986. **Die Geburt des Gottkönigs. Studien zur Überlieferung eines altägyptischen Mythos**. Wiesbaden: Otto Harrassowitz.

Butler, J. 1990. **Gender Trouble. Feminism and the Subversion of Identity**. New York and London: Routledge.

Butler, J. 1993. **Bodies that Matter. On the discursive limits of "sex"**. London: Routledge.

Cooper, J. 2011. The geographic and cosmographic expression tA-nTr. **The Bulletin of the Australian Centre for Egyptology**, 22, 47–66.

Coyette, A. 2015. La naissance merveilleuse d'Hatshepsout dans les reliefs de Deir el-Bahari. In C. Cannuyer et C. Vialle eds. **Les naissances merveilleuses en Orient. Jacques Vermeylen (1942-2014) in memoriam**. Bruxelles: Société belge d'études orientales, 87–112.

Dorman, P. F. 2014. Innovation at the Dawn of the New Kingdom. In J. M. Galán, B. M. Bryan and P. F. Dorman eds. **Creativity and Innovation in the Reign of Hatshepsut. Papers from the Theban Workshop 2010**. Studies in Ancient Oriental Civilization 69. Chicago: The Oriental Institute of the

University of Chicago, 1–6.

Detienne, M. 1994. **The Gardens of Adonis. Spices in Greek Mythology**. Princeton: Princeton University Press.

DuQuesne, T. 2005. The Spiritual and the Sexual in Ancient Egypt. **Discussions in Egyptology**, 61, 7–24.

El-Awady, T. 2009. **Sahure-the pyramid causeway. History and decoration program in the Old Kingdom**. Abusir XVI. Prague: Charles University in Prague.

Espinel, A. D. 2017. The scents of Punt (and elsewhere): trade and function of *snṯr* and *ꜥntw* during the Old Kingdom. In I. Incordino and P. P. Creasman eds. **Flora Trade Between Egypt and Africa in Antiquity**. Oxford: Oxbow, 21–47.

Fahlander, F. 2008. Differences that matter. Materialities, material culture and social practice. In H. Glørstad and L. Hedeager eds. **Six Essays on the Materiality of Society and Culture**. Lindome: Bricoleur Press, 127–154.

Fahlander, F. 2012. Facing gender. Corporeality, materiality, intersectionality and resurrection. In I.-M. B. Danielsson and S. Thedéen eds. **To Tender Gender: The Pasts and Futures of Gender Research**. Stockholm: Stockholm University, 137–152.

Farina, G. 1924. Le vocali dell'antico egiziano. **Aegyptus**, 5, 4, 313–325.

Finnestad, R. B. 1997. Temples of the Ptolemaic and Roman Periods: Ancient Traditions in New Contexts. In B. E. Shafer ed. **Temples of Ancient Egypt**. Ithaca and London: ornell University Press, 185–237.

Frandsen, P. J. 1997. On Categorization and Metaphorical Structuring: Some Remarks on Egyptian Art and Language. **Cambridge Archaeological Journal**, 7, 1, 71–104.

Gabolde, L. 2014. Hatshepsut at Karnak: A Woman under God's Commands. In J. M. Galán, B. M. Bryan and P. F. Dorman eds. **Creativity and Innovation in the Reign of Hatshepsut**. Papers from the Theban Workshop 2010. Chicago: The Oriental Institute of the University of Chicago, 33–48.

Gardiner, A. H. 1937. **Late-Egyptian Miscellanies**. Bruxelles: Fondation Égyptologique Reine Élisabeth.

Gardiner, A. H. 1950. ΟΝΝΩΦΡΙΣ. **Miscellanea Academica Berolinensia** II, 2, 44–53.

Gitton, M. 1984. **Les divines épouses de la 18ᵉ dynastie**. Centre de Recherches d'Histoire Ancienne 61. Paris: Annales Littéraires de l'Université de Besançon.

Goedicke, H. 1960. **Die Stellung des Königs im Alten Reich**. Wiesbaden: Harrassowitz.

Graeber, D. 2015. Radical alterity is just another way of saying "reality". A reply to Eduardo Viveiros de Castro. **Hau: Journal of Ethnographic Theory**, 5 (2), 1–41

Grimal, N.-Ch. 1986. **Les termes de la propagande royale égyptienne de la XIXe Dynastie à la conquête d'Alexandre**. Paris: Institut de France.

Hallmann, S. 2006. **Die Tributszenen des Neuen Reiches**. Ägypten und Altes Testament 66. Wiesbaden.

Hamilakis, Y. 2013. **Archaeology and the Senses. Human Experience, Memory and Affect**. Cambridge: Cambridge University Press.

Harvey, S. 2003. Interpreting Punt: Geographic, Cultural and Artistic Landscapes. In D. O'Connor and S. Quirke eds. **Mysterious Lands**. London: UCL Press, 81–92.

Helck, W. 1961. **Urkunden der 18. Dynastie. Übersetzung zu den Heften 17-22**. Berlin: Akademie Verlag.

Hornung, E. 1982. **Conceptions of God in Ancient Egypt. The One and the Many**. London and Melbourne: Routledge & Kegan Paul.

Hsu, S.-W. 2014. The images of love: The use of figurative expressions in ancient Egyptian Love Songs. **Orientalia**, NS 83 (4), 407–416.

Ingold, T. 2007. Materials against materiality. **Archaeological dialogues**, 14 (1), 1–16.

Inconnu-Bocquillon, D. 2001. **Le mythe de la Déesse Lointaine à Philae**. Bibliothèque d'Étude 132 Cairo: Institut Français d'Archéologie Orientale.

Iwaszczuk, J. 2014. The Legacy of Senwosret I During the Reign of Hatshepsut and Thutmose III. **Études et Travaux**, XXVII, 162–178.

Joyce, R. A. 2015. Transforming Archaeology, Transforming Materiality. **Archeological Papers of the American Anthropological Association**, 26, 181–191.

Kjølby, A. 2009. Material Agency, Attribution and Experience of Agency in Ancient Egypt. The case of New Kingdom private temple statues. In R. Nyord and A. Kjølby eds. **'Being in Ancient Egypt' Thoughts on Agency, Materiality and Cognition. Proceedings of the seminar held in Copenhagen, September 29-30, 2006**. BAR International Series 2019. Oxford: Archaeopress, 31–46.

Knappett, C. 2014. Materiality in Archaeological Theory. In C. Smith ed. **Encyclopedia of Global Archaeology**. New York: Springer, 4700–4708.

Leitz, C. et al. 2002. **Lexikon der Ägyptischen Götter und Götterbezeichnungen. Band V. ḫ-ḥ**. Orientalia Lovaniensia Analecta 114. Leuven: Uitgeverij Peeters.

Marshall, Y. and Alberti, B. 2014. A Matter of Difference: Karen Barad, Ontology and Archaeological Bodies. **Cambridge Archaeological Journal**, 24, 1, 19–36.

Matić, U. 2016. (De)queering Hatshepsut. Binary bind in archaeology of Egypt and kingship beyond the corporeal. **Journal of Archaeological Method and Theory**, 23: 810-831.

Megahed, M. and Vymazalová, H. 2015. The South Saqqara Circumcision Scene: a Fragment of an Old Kingdom Birth-Legend. In F. Coppens, J. Janák and H. Vymazalová eds. **Royal versus Divine Authority. Acquisition, Legitimization and Renewal of Power**. 7th Symposium on Egyptian Royal Ideology. Prague, June 26-28, 2013. Königtum, Staat und Gesellschaft früher Hochkulturen 4, 4. Wiesbaden: Harrassowitz Verlag, 275–287.

Meeks, D. 2003. Locating Punt. In D. O'Connor and S. Quirke eds. **Mysterious Lands**. London: UCL Press, 53–80.

Meskell, L. 2004. **Object Worlds in Ancient Egypt: Material Biographies Past and Present**. Oxford: Berg.

Meskell, L. 2005. Introduction: Object Orientations. In L. Meskell, ed. **Archaeologies of Materiality**. Oxford: Blackwell, 1–17.

Miller, D. 2005. Materiality: An Introduction. In D. Miller ed. **Materiality**. Durham and London: Duke University Press, 1–50.

Münster, M. 1968. **Untersuchungen zur Göttin Isis vom Alten Reich bis zum Ende des Neuen Reiches**. Berlin: Verlag Bruno Hessling.

Myśliwiec, K. 2004. **Eros on the Nile**. Translated from Polish by Geoffrey L. Packer. Ithaca: Cornell University Press.

Naville, E. 1897. **The Temple of Deir el Bahari II**. London: The Egypt Exploration Fund.

Navillle, E. 1898. **The Temple of Deir el Bahari III**. London: The Egypt Exploration Fund.

Nusier, M. K., Bataineh, H. N., Bataineh, Z. M and Daradka, H. M. 2007. Effect of Frankincense (Boswellia thurifera) on Reproductive System in Adult Male Rat. **Journal of Health Science**, 53, 4, 365–370.

Oppenheim, A. 2011. The Early Life of Pharaoh: Divine Birth and Adolescence Scenes in the Causeway of Senwosret III at Dahshur. In M. Bárta, F. Coppens, and J. Krejčí eds. **Abusir and Saqqara in the Year 2010/2011**. Prague: Czech Institute for Egyptology, Faculty of Arts, Charles University in Prague, 171–188.

Perry, E. M. and Joyce, R. A. 2001. Providing a Past for "Bodies That Matter": Judith Butler's Impact on the Archaeology of Gender. **International Journal of Sexuality and Gender Studies**, 6 (1/2), 63–76.

Posener, G. 1960. **De la divinité du pharaon**. Paris: Cahiers de la Société Asiatique.

Povinelli, E. A. 2006. **The Empire of Love. Toward a Theory of Intimacy, Genealogy, and Carnality**. Durham and London: Duke University Press.

Quack, J. F. 2010. How unapproachable is a Pharaoh? In G-B. Lanfrachi and R. Rollinger eds. **Concepts of Kingship in Antiquity. Proceedings of the European Science Foundation exploratory Workshop held in Padova, November 28th-December 1st, 2007**. Padova: S.A.R.G.O.N. Editrice e Libreria, 1–14.

Quack, J. F. 2017. Ägyptische Einflüsse auf nordwestsemitische Königspräsentationen? In C. Levin und R. Müller eds. **Herrschaftslegitimation in vorderorientalischen Reichen der Eisenzeit**. Tübingen: Mohr Siebeck, 1–66.

Rikala, M. 2008. Sacred Marriage in the New Kingdom of Ancient Egypt Circumstantial Evidence for a Ritual Interpretation. In M. Nissinen and R. Uro eds. **Sacred Marriages. The Divine-Human Sexual Metaphor from Sumer to Early Christianity**. Winona Lake: Eisenbrauns, 115–144.

Reineke, W. 1984. Heft 7. Historisch-biographische Urkunden von Zeitgenossen der Hatschepsut=Nr. 150 bis Nr. 178. In E. Blumenthal, I. Müller, W. F. Reineke eds. **Urkunden der 18. Dynastie. Übersetzung zu den Heften 5-16**. Berlin: Akademie Verlag, 86–123.

Rummel, U. 2016. Der Leib der Göttin: Materialität und Semantik ägyptischer Felslandschaft. In S. Beck, B. Backes, I-T. Liao, H. Simon, A. Verbovsek eds. **Gebauter Raum: Architektur-Landschaft-Mensch**. Beiträge des fünften Münchner Arbeitskreises Junge Ägyptologie (MAJA 5) 12.12. bis

14.12.2014. Göttinger Orientforschungen IV. 62. Wiesbaden: Harrassowitz, 41–74.

Schneider, T. 1997. Beiträge zur sogennanten "Neueren Komparatistik" **Lingua Aegyptia. Journal of Egyptian Language Studies**, 5, 189–209.

Schukraft, B. 2007. Homosexualität im Alten Ägypten. **Studien zur Altägyptischen Kultur**, 36, 297–331.

Stock, H. 1951. **NTr nfr-der gute Gott?** Hildesheim: Gebr. Gerstenberg Verlag.

Takács, G. 1999. **Etymological Dictionary of Egyptian. Volume One: A Phonological Introduction**. Handbuck der Orientalistik I. Leiden: Brill.

Taterka, F. 2016. Hatshepsut's expedition to the land of Punt-novelty or tradition? In C. Alvarez, A. Belekdanian, A-K. Gill and S. Klein eds. **Current Research in Egyptology 2015. Proceedings of the Sixteenth Annual Symposium University of Oxford 2015**. Oxford: Oxbow Books, 114–123.

Taterka, F. 2017a. Kraina Punt - Ziemia Boga starożytnych Egipcjan. In D. Lewandowska, H. Rajfura eds. **Ziemia Obiecana & Panta rhei - Pamięć, czas i przemijanie w starożytności**. Schole 13. Warszawa: Wydawnictwo Naukowe Sub Lupa, Koło Starożytnicze UW, 37–49.

Taterka, F. 2017b. **Opowieści znad Nilu. Opowiadania egipskie z okresu Średniego Państwa. Ze zwojów papirusowych, tabliczek drewnianych i ostrakonów zebrał, przełożył, wstępem i komentarzem opatrzył**. Warszawa: Agade.

Tilley, C. 2004. **The Materiality of Stone. Explorations in Landscape Phenomenology**. Oxford: Berg.

Tilley, C. 2007. Materiality in materials. **Archaeological Dialogues**, 14, 16–20.

Verbovsek, A. and Backes, B. 2015. Sinne und Sinnlichkeit in den ägyptischen Liebesliedern. In H. Navratilova and R. Langráfová eds. **Sex and the Golden Goddess II. World of the Love Songs**. Prague: Charles University, 105–119.

Vernus, P. 1995. **Essai sur la conscience de l'histoire dans l'Egypte pharaonique**. Paris: H. Champion.

Viveiros de Castro, E. 2015. **The Relative Native. Essays on Indigenous Conceptual Worlds**. Chicago: HAU.

von Lieven, A. 2004. Das Göttliche in der Natur erkennen. Tiere, Pflanzen und Phänomene der unbelebten Natur als Manifestationen des Göttlichen (mit einer Edition der Baumliste P. Berlin 29027). **Zeitschrift für ägyptische Sprache und Altertumskunde**, 131, 156-172.

von Lieven, A. 2013. Jungfräuliche Mütter? Eine ägyptologische Perspektive. In Th. Södling Hgg. **Zu Bethlehem geboren? Das Jesus-Buch Benedikts XVI. und die Wissenschaft**. Theologie kontrovers. Freiburg: Herder, 156–170.

von Lieven, A. 2016. »Thy Fragrance is in all my Limbs« On the Olfactory Sense in Ancient Egyptian Religion. In P. Reichling and M. Strothmann eds. **Religion für die Sinne**. Oberhausen: Athena Verlag, 309–325.

Walker, J. H. 1996. **Studies in Ancient Egyptian Anatomical Terminology**. The Australian Centre for Egyptology 4. Wiltshire: Aris and Phillips Ltd.

Wilson, P. 1997. **A Ptolemaic Lexikon. A Lexicographical Study of the Texts in the Temple of Edfu**. Orientalia Lovaniensia Analecta 78. Leuven: Peeters.

Texts, materiality and agency in Middle Kingdom literature

Érika Maynart

Introduction

In this article, I analyse the material form of texts based on two examples from the Middle Kingdom considered here as textual objects: the stela of Sehetep-ib-re and the writing tablet containing the Complaints of Kha-kheper-re-seneb. The ancient Egyptian literature was traditionally transmitted orally, overemphasising the immaterial origin of the words we read from Egyptian papyri and other supports of textual evidence. Here I propose the reading of such textual objects as social and material practices of writing that were both formed and shaped by human performances.

Composition and transmission of texts: the relationship between form and performance

The practical impact of a text on an individual's performance is directly related with the form provided by the scribe to the manuscript. This has guided a number of analyses regarding the function of writings (Grimal 1984, 17). We can thus notice two ways in which agency works in the process of transmission of a written message: on the one hand, the agency of the writer creates the text in its material and textual wholeness, on the other, the agency of the text acts upon society. The writing process was motivated by a certain number of intentions, some of which we can infer from the written registers. In order to do so, we must first consider the material agency of the writings, as has recently been argued, especially in *Agency in Ancient Writing*, edited by Joshua Englehardt (2013). The contributors to this volume agree that it is clear that writings equally belong to the group of material and documental record. Thus, the development of an approach that contemplates both aspects of textual sources, is an important task, as textuality and materiality are complementary and mutually informative. The notion of agency, as open to different definitions as it currently is, can contribute to the undoing of the divisions between agents and structures, between what is human and what is a material object. 'Individual action is thus contextualised within structures that are at once created through agentive practice and themselves provide identity and meaning to the practices of social actors' (Englehardt and Nakassis 2013, 4). The invisibility of specific social agents is most often an obstacle to studies about the past, but texts are an exception, as they specifically provide means to inform us about their agents in ways that could not be explored archaeologically (Englehardt and Nakassis 2013, 6).

Approaching writings materially is a relatively recent trend and recovers some inherently textual characteristics that have somehow been neglected by scholarship. Traditional approaches to textual sources have contributed to reinforce and maintain the thesis that textual records are opposed to other material records—an assumption usually based on the documentality of texts. In our historical, archaeological and philological traditions a sole function of carrying out information and abstract ideas formulated by language is attributed to written documents. Instead, the material approach of textual sources emphasise the materialisation of language provided by texts, and their ability of making language visible and apprehensible through the senses, in order to ensure the permanence of the meanings one wishes to communicate (Kelber 1997, 19; Assmann 2006; Baines 2007).

Studies on the codified forms of ancient texts also have focused mainly on the development of writing systems and languages, as well as their changes and eventual disappearance (Baines et al 2008; Houston 2012). Such studies also insufficiently explore the material form of texts. On the other hand, some recent studies have analysed the form of the texts considering the materials that make them tangible, therefore bringing texts to the physical world, where they also exist materially. This is crucial for the text to fulfil its purpose in society, which is spreading its message.

Texts, materiality and agency

For us to recognise that writing is "fundamentally material" we must consider texts as objects beforehand (Whitehouse and Piquette 2013, passim). In the case of literary texts, emphasis is usually given to its immaterial origin in a fundamentally oral culture as Middle Kingdom Egypt. Literary texts found in papyri, ostraca and stelae were likely widespread among Egyptian people, including the illiterate majority. The contents of written texts were transmitted orally, making texts part of an integrating general knowledge that served as background for the constitution of communities and constituted a group of commonplaces in the oral Egyptian culture that were transmitted regardless of the acquisition of literacy. Literacy comes from previous non-literate sign language systems, which are founded on more general and universal cognitive abilities such as the ability to recognise and name objects (Smith, 2013, 75). In emerging writing systems, the constitution of literacy trains the recognition of signs in a more 'word-like' form, instead of being only 'object-like'. The transition from object-like forms of assimilation to semantic ones allows us to blur the strict line between literate and non-literate audiences, since emergent writing systems such as hieroglyphs should not be seen as creations of the genius of some exceptional people. Rather it is as a technological process that meets certain social demands that are not limited to high culture use. The wide use of textual amulets in ancient Egypt is an indicator of this process (Dieleman, 2015). The very nature of Egyptian writing systems was that of being formed by images. A huge range of images allowed Egyptians to read interpreting multiple semantic possibilities from an object, a gesture or action, for example (Loprieno 2004).

Therefore, an Egyptian literary text is a codified version of socially established cultural knowledge that used to be communicated only through direct communication, *vis-à-vis*, between speakers and their audience: individuals who used to narrate, tell or sing a story, song or poem for those who listened. Written composition became a reality after an individual or a group codified a given text. But before being codified narratives, songs, poems, hymns and sayings are texts in the sense of a semantic unity: a unity of cultural meaning elaborated by language (Assmann 2006). Non-written texts were transmitted and acknowledged orally. In order to codify them, specific literate agents had necessarily to deal with materials and produce a real object that could be read (Derchain 1996). Thus writing is a material practice, and texts should be methodologically considered. We must have this basic empirical understanding of ancient literary texts in mind in order to treat them methodologically as cultural objects.

The process of materialising language through writing aims to stabilise the meaning of what one communicates. Thus the development of technologies required in the materialisation of cultural meanings as texts takes place. These cultural meanings include notational, numerical and administrative information on the first economic records available today. Writing is a technological achievement, a social tool made possible by the creative use of natural resources to meet the demands of recording. In Haas words, "writing always takes place in a material context, it employs material tools and produces material artefacts" which operate socially through agency (Hass 1996, 4).

The way we conceive texts is largely informed by the physical interactions we establish with texts and writing tools. The physical presence of a text directly impacts the perception of a writer upon what Haas understands as the 'sense of the text' (Haas 1996, 118). The sense of the text must be understood as how one comprehends and makes a mental representation of the text. A writer who possesses three-dimensional writing tools such as pen and paper develops a broader apprehension about its own writing than a writer who uses a computer—especially due to the fact that virtual technology only enables a two-dimensional connection between writer and text. Even though this is not Haas main argument, the question on whether the development of a virtual writing technology deprived us from the physical perception of a text, conditioning us to the abstract conception of texts we have been practicing, remains of interest. Besides, this virtual interface has possibly contributed to an even deeper serialization of the text, from its composition by an author to an editor, reviewer, translator, and finally to its distribution, which often comes through a digital version. The digital use of texts is a consequence from the ever-growing relation between individuals and electronic devices. These processes contribute to increase the distance between reader and text, even though we must admit that reading still depends on material objects that allow two-dimensional visual contact (or even hearing) through electronic devices such as tablets, smartphones and notebooks.

In the last 20 years, the distance and different approaches from archaeology and philology have culminated in the process of a 'dematerialization' of writing (Whitehouse and Piquette 2013, 2). While philology was concerned with the interpretation of texts and linguistic analysis, archaeology developed methodologies to uncover and report archaeological contexts where textual objects were found as well as to preserve its record. However, it did not treat texts as objects of the past in the archaeological analysis of records, but as testimonies about the past. History also contributed to the dematerialisation of texts by emphasising the 'documentalising' aspect of texts across many years of disciplinary tradition. Moreover, editions and translations of primary textual sources have prioritised the presentation of texts in their codified completion, depriving the sources from its physical wholeness. This is the case of main compilations and anthologies of Pharaonic literature produced by Egyptology. Following Whitehouse and Piquette's approach, studies on the materiality of texts are much more meaningful when aware of the relationship between content and context—archaeological, historical, and cultural—regarding the physical and social environment in which the manuscripts were conceived as a material practice of an ancient everyday life. In other words, a materiality approach to texts aims to break with the notion that considers texts as 'immaterial sources about the past' (Whitehouse and Piquette 2013, 2; Piquette 2013, 216). Rather, texts are products of the past, produced as result of active human interactions with their context, and active (re)producers of culture, according to an epistemological role referred by Moreland (Moreland 2001; 2006; Englehardt and Nakassis 2013, 7). As defended by Englehardt and Nakassis,

"[...] from an agency approach social practices are historical processes, not merely their consequences (Pauketat 2001, 74). In the course of writing a document, an individual necessarily makes use of a wide variety of structures—linguistic, of course, but also administrative, economic, ideological, and so on—that may be reproduced or changed while instantiated in the process of textual production. The result is that detailed studies such as those made possible by early writing provide important insights into social structures and macro-historical processes" (Englehardt and Nakassis 2013, 7).

The more 'holistic' approach argued by Englehardt and Nakassis is part of the 'material turn' of texts since the latter half of the 1990's. The main purpose is to readdress the relationship between materiality and textuality, which has been lost in the context of scholarly traditions and was much more natural to the perception of human agents in ancient times. The comprehension of written records must go beyond studies about the textual meaning contained in texts. In other words, one must understand textual objects not as texts on objects.

Approaching writing as a material practice allows us to analyse both the individuals' agency involved in the composition and the agency of the text itself. Composition is fundamentally material as it relies on the material practice of human agents that elaborated, through the creation and production of writing, certain performances of writing, reading, reciting and listening. Composition also relies on the social agency of textual objects, which influence the way writing is conducted. In regard of literary texts in general, and more specifically the 'instructions' or *sbayt* (Lichtheim 1996), it is possible to analyse in which ways a textual object acts in the training of human performances, e.g. reading and hearing. This is an important point to highlight if one intends to analyse overly neglected dramatic aspects such as rhythm, metrics, parallelism, assonance and alliteration. These aspects act as basic repetitions, partially mimicking the same repetitions that occur in spoken language, but mainly operate as mnemotechnical devices for remembering the text and facilitate reading (Eyre and Baines 1989; Loprieno 2000).

The emphasis on the agency of texts works as a guide to its performance of reading, though it does not explore all the possibilities of interaction textual objects establish in society. Agency alone does not allow us to think concretely about a broader dissemination of textual contents, as it is widely accepted that instructions became a commonplace in the Middle Kingdom. In this regard, Eyre (2013) argues that Assmann (1995; 2003) and Loprieno (2000) overemphasised the level of sophistication in the composition of literary works. These works would demand from the reader a very deep comprehension of the writing system and of how writing was able to determine a certain way of reading, thus narrowing the reality of textual communication and making it quantitatively determined by literacy. Eyre (2013, 101–142 specially 105 and 141–142) attributes to both authors the characterisation of written language as something determined by an Egyptian 'literocracy' (Assmman 2003, 48) that worked to reach a level of finesse (Loprieno 2000, 138) of the Egyptian language through writing. According to this idea, the more sophisticated writing practices became, the more specialisation was required from readers. Therefore, a restricted number of readers would be affected by the content communicated, in disregard to the different uses of literacy that Der Manuelian treats as levels of literacy (Manuelian 1999; see also Lemos, in this volume). It does not make much sense if we take into account one of the ultimate goals of written language, which is the stabilisation of words in time so they could be better controlled and received, in a process of solidification of culture (Eyre 2013, 108–109). According to Eyre, it is preferable to refer to a 'hearing' of Egyptian literature than to a 'reading' of it. Thus, the repetition of words and sounds in a text would be much more bound to the hearing perception. Anyone who had memorised a given text could recite it and hear it, and anyone who could listen would have been a potential agent in the process of textual transmission.

Two textual objects in perspective

Textual agency operates largely through the image constituted by the combination of materials and the writing system's image. Pascal Vernus refers to the relationship between texts and supports for continuity purposes as a symbiotic unit, a notion that we extend to all manuscripts but avoid to separate the textual object in support and text (Vernus 2011). All technologies applied to writing produce an object that necessarily informs the reader through some sensorial ways that are stimulated by the whole object, being it a book, a wall, a vase or a document written in Braille system. The technological achievement of making writing in the Ancient Near East combined art and writing systems in many ways, using different tools and materials in order to produce meaning (Schmandt-Besserat 2007). An Egyptian stela, for example, is not just a carved stone made into a display in which a text is shown. Let us examine the stela of Sehetep-ib-re, currently held at the Cairo Museum (Cairo 20538). The stela comes from Abydos, and it measures 123cm x 48cm x 24cm (Lichtheim 2006, 125).

Lichtheim classified Sehetep-ib-re's stela as a funerary stela (Lichtheim 2006, 125–126). Contrarily, Derchain (1996, 84–5) considers it as a celebratory monument in homage of a mission to Abydos led by

Sehetep-ib-re, a Middle Kingdom dignitary and employee of the royal treasure during the reigns of Senusret III and Amenemhet III. The stela became famous as the oldest record available of the Loyalist Instruction. There are other 70 copies of the Instruction, all dating to the New Kingdom. The text is known for the emphatic statement of the need for worshipping Amenemhet III in order to secure a peaceful life:

"Beginning of the teaching that he made to his children.

I will say something important and have you hear;

I will let you know the method of continuity,

the system of living correctly, of conducting a lifetime in peace.

Worship the king—Nimaatre, alive forever—

in your innermost beings,

associate his incarnation with your minds.

He is Perception, which is in hearts,

for his eyes probe every torso.

He is the Sun, by whose rays one sees;

how much more illuminating of the Two Lands is he than the sundisk!

How much more freshening is he than a high inundation,

for he has filled the Two Lands with the force of life […]." (Allen 2014, 157)

Although this starts the most well-known excerpt from inscription on the stela, other parts of the text include eulogies and self-praises and a brief biography of Sehetep-ib-re (Lichtheim 2006, 125–129). In addition to the texts, there are images on both sides of the stela on the top, and an image of Sehetep-ib-re below, besides the verse. Translations of the Loyalist Instruction have been published in various occasions (Gardiner 1909; Allen 2014). However, these referential publications do not do a comprehensive study of all aspects the stela, considered as a material and textual object.

Although this is the most notable example of a text that contains the name of its possible author, Derchain argues that the reference to Sehetep-ib-re is an intellectual one. It means that his initiative to spread an already familiar text at Abydos makes him an authority capable of assuring the local meaning of these teachings and its following reception. We can imagine that someone would eventually read these teachings audibly in public, and the stela might have been a sort of landmark, materialising the memory of Sehetep-ib-re and his intention to disseminate the sayings of the Loyalist Instruction. These moments, though probably scarce, could take place during festivities, in which recitations were very common (Eyre 2013, 120–122; 125–127). The intention was to spread the written content to as many people as possible, and every time that people who had already heard the instructions passed by the location of the stela they would remember Sehetep-ib-re, the instructions and the connection between the two established by the stela, instigated and updated. Individuals facing the stela interacted with a textual and pictorial object. The relationship between images and the text then becomes an interesting aspect of the social role of objects and texts. But we can also analyse the presence of images on the stela that were related to the text. Bryan approached this theme as a disjunction between both text and image (Bryan 1996, 161–168). According to the author, messages transmitted by images and texts targeted different audiences, both literate and illiterate people. By analysing a stela from Abydos during the 23rd Dynasty and some other examples very similar to the stela of Sehetep-ib-re, Bryan argues that images do not always confirm what is expressed in the text and vice-versa. Even though we believe one should not make a polarised distinction between the types of audience that interacted with textual objects such as the stela of Sehetep-ib-re. Bryan's conclusion on the function of an object containing both text and image is precise: one may not necessarily explain the other.

The problem is that 'only monuments showed a deliberate form of written publication' (Eyre 2013, 139). However, most instructions composed during the Middle Kingdom were not published in stelae. One example is the writing tablet containing the Complaints of Kha-kheper-re-seneb (British Museum EA5645; Shaw and Nicholson 1995, 164; Lichteim 2006, 145–149; Parkinson 1997; Gardiner 1909). The text was written on a board covered with stucco, which measures 30.1cm x 55.7cm x 0.8cm; and weighs 1.1kg. Its weight is comparable to some modern portable computers. Unlike the Loyalist Instruction, the Complaints of Kha-kheper-re-seneb are written in hieratic and do not show any praise or eulogy neither to monarchs nor to the individual to which the authorship of the text is attributed in the exordium.

Put by some authors in the roster of the so-called Egyptian "pessimistic literature", the Complaints of Kha-kheper-re-seneb describe the changes in the social life in Egypt that deeply disturb the narrator. The sayings delineate a chaotic and turbulent panorama found all over the country due to greed, corruption and death. The disturbed narrator seeks advice from his own heart. The text refers to the 12th and 13th Dynasties, but the object in which the text was written dates from the middle of the 18th Dynasty. A part of the same text (EA5645 recto 10–11) is also conserved in an ostracon in the Cairo Museum (Parkinson 1997). There are only two artefacts materialising this composition to this date, but the acknowledgement of Kha-kheper-re-seneb is documented in the papyrus Chester Beatty IV (EA10684, 3; Gardiner 1935, vol. 1 28–44) among other great scribes.

Evidently, the agency of a text such as this, considering its physical shape, is quite different. In order to assess the profusion of written texts, one must first take into account that the Egyptian written culture was a copyist one, and that many individuals were involved in the production of these textual objects in daily life. In such a context, the processes of composition and publishing cannot be considered separately, since for the very acquisition of literacy one must have created its texts and kept small collections (Eyre 2013). The portability of this tablet as well as the faster writing allowed by hieratic system show the necessity of making writing and reading a frequent practice for someone (or some group), and its physical characteristics indicate a certain expectation of durability in its daily use—something that would not be suitable in the case of a papyrus and would not be supported by a small ostracon.

Conclusion

There is no material evidence to support that the Egyptians privileged text transmission on particularised objects such as the writing tablet. However, a monument such as a stela is a comparatively worse way of optimising frequent readings or auditions. Texts were written to be performed, and a monumental text such as the one on the stela of Sehetep-ib-re would demand from the individual reader some effort to remain stand in front of the monument to execute the performance required by the textual object. Against this inconvenience, the particularisation of the text into a smaller and more portable object would provide more autonomy to the scribe, who is usually the very redactor/copyist of the texts in his possession. The attribution of being a redactor comes with some responsibility over the transmission of the text, embodied by the scribe in his oral performances. Therefore, writing is a social and material practice considering the bodily actions of producing and reading it (Bennet 2013), as the text function is that of remaining intimately connected to culture. Confronting the Loyalist Instruction translations by Lichtheim (1973) and Allen (2014) with the hieroglyphic text (Allen 2014), I prefer to maintain a type of translation reliable to the figures of speech in the source, in which the concreteness of the sayings points to the embodiment of a religious performance, for example in the expression 'in your bodies' (*m ḥnw n ḥwt.tn*) instead of 'in your innermost beings' as translated by Allen. If we consider this, we read the text as 'Worship the King— Nimaatre alive forever—in your bodies', so the text makes itself a device to remind subjects about the corporeity of body performances at the very moment of the reading performance.

In Middle Kingdom Egypt, the boundaries between text and image were less strict than the ones established by the modern thought. A text is always embodied through some material object that provides a tangible image to guide the performance of individuals, either literate or illiterate. Therefore, an image could be manipulated in order to become more verbal and fulfil certain functions that writing alone could not. This does not authorise us, however, to approach textual objects exclusively through the lens of textuality without exploring the full potential of those sources.

References

Allen, J. 2014. **Middle Egyptian Literature**. London: Cambridge University Press.

Assmann, J. 1999. Cultural and literary texts. In: Gerald Moers ed. **Definitely: Egyptian literature. Proceedings of the Symposion "Ancient Egyptian Literature - History and Forms"**. Göttingen: Lingua Aegyptia: Studia Monographica 2, 1-15.

Assmann, J. 2003. **The mind of Egypt: history and meaning in the time of the pharaohs**. Cambridge (Mass.): Harvard University Press.

Assmann, J. 2006. Form as a mnemonic device. In, R. Horseley, J. Draper and J. Foley eds. Performing the Gospel. **Orality, Memory, and Mark**. Minneapolis: Fortress, 67–82.

Baines, J. 2007. **Visual and Written Culture in Ancient Egypt**. Oxford: Oxford University Press.

Baines, J., J. Bennet and S. Houston. 2008. **The Disappearance of Writing Systems: Perspectives on Literacy and Communication**. London: Equinox Publishing.

Bennet, J. 2013. Epilogue. In: Piquette, K. and Whitehouse, R. eds. **Writing as Material Practice: Substance, surface and medium**. London: Ubiquity Press, 335-342.

Bryan, B. 1996. The disjunction of text and image in Egyptian art. In: P. Der Manuelian ed. **Studies in Honor of William Kelly Simpson**, Vol. 1. Boston: Museum of Fine Arts, 161–168.

Derchain, P. 1996. Auteur et societé. In A. Loprieno ed. **Ancient Egyptian Literature: History and Forms**. Leiden: Brill, 83–94.

Dieleman, J. 2015. The materiality of textual amulets in ancient Egypt. In D. Boschung and J. N. Bremmer eds. **The materiality of magic**. Paderborn: Wilhelm Fink, 23–58.

Englehardt, J. ed. 2013. **Agency in Ancient Writing**. Boulder: University Press of Colorado.

Englehardt, J. and D. Nakassis. 2013. Individual Intentionality, Social Structure, and Material Agency in

Early Writing and Emerging Script Technologies. In J. Englehardt ed. **Agency in Ancient Writing**. Boulder: University Press of Colorado.

Eyre, C. and Baines, J. 1989. Interactions between Orality and Literacy in Ancient Egypt. In: Schoulsboe, K. and Larsen, M. T. eds. **Literacy and Society**. Copenhagen: Akademisk Forlag. 91-119.

Eyre, C. 2013. The Practice of Literature: The Relationship between Content, Form, Audience, and Performance. In: R. Enmarch and V. Lepper eds. **Ancient Egyptian Literature: Theory and Practice**. London: The British Academy, 101–142.

Gardiner, A. 1909. **The Admonitions of an Egyptian sage from a hieratic papyrus in Leiden**. Leipzig: J. C. Hinrichs.

Gardiner, A. 1935. **Hieratic papyri in the British Museum: III series. Chester Beatty Gift**. Vol. 1. London: British Museum Press.

Grimal, P. 1984. Préface. In C. Lalouette. **Textes Sacrés et Textes Profanes de l'Ancienne Égypte**. Vol. 2. Paris: Gallimard, 7–19.

Haas, C. 1996. **Writing Technology: studies on the materiality of literacy**. Mahwah, NJ: Lawrence Erlbaum.

Kelber, W. 1997 [1983]. **The Oral and The Written Gospel**. Bloomington; Indianapolis: Indiana University Press.

Lichtheim, M. 2006 [1973]. **Ancient Egyptian Literature.** Vol. 1: The Old and Middle Kingdoms. Berkeley: University of California Press.

Lichtheim, M. 1996. Didactic Literature. In A. Loprieno. **Ancient Egyptian Literature: History and Forms**. Leiden: Brill, 243–62.

Loprieno, Antonio. 2000. **La pensée et l'écriture: Pour une analyse sémiotique de la culture égyptienne**. Paris: Cybelle.

Loprieno, Antonio. 2004. **Ancient Egyptian: A linguistic introduction**. Cambridge: Cambridge University Press.

Manuelian, P. Der. 1999. Semi-literacy in Ancient Egypt; Some Examples from the Amarna Period. In **Gold of Praise. Studies on Ancient Egypt in Honor of Edward F. Wente**. Chicago: Oriental Institute. 285–98.

Moreland, J. 2001. **Archaeology and Text**. London: Duckworth.

Moreland, J. 2006. Archaeology and Texts: Subservience or Enlightenment. **Annual Review of Anthropology**. 35, 135–151.

Parkinson, R. 1997. The Text of Khakheperreseneb: new readings of EA 5645, and an unpublished ostracon. **Journal of Egyptian Archaeology**, 83, 55–68.

Piquette, K. E. 2013. It Is Written?: Making, remaking and unmaking early 'writing' in the lower Nile Valley. In: Piquette, K. E. and Whitehouse, R. D. eds. **Writing as Material Practice: Substance, surface and medium**. 213-238. London: Ubiquity Press.

Whitehouse, R. and Piquette, K. 2013. Introduction: Developing an approach to writing as material practice. In: Piquette, K. E. and Whitehouse, R. D. eds. **Writing as Material Practice:**

Substance, surface and medium. 1-13. London: Ubiquity Press.

Shaw, I. and P. Nicholson. 1995. **The British Museum dictionary of ancient Egypt**. London: British Museum Press.

Smith, A. 2013. Are Writing Systems Intelligently Designed? In J. Englehardt ed. **Agency in Ancient Writing**. Boulder: University Press of Colorado, 71–93.

Vernus, P. 2011. "Littérature", "littéraire" et supports d'écriture. Contribution à une théorie de la littérature dans l'Égypte pharaonique. In: **Egyptian and Egyptological Documents, Archives, Libraries II**. Milan: Pontremoli. 19–146.

"All that glitters is not gold": the symbolism and materiality of Egyptian funerary amulets

Carmen Muñoz Pérez

Introduction

Funerary amulets are precious, though underestimated, sources for the study of the Egyptian culture. On the one hand, the analysis of tombs is very useful for archaeologists as archaeological contexts preserve the motionless last instant of use of past objects through time. On the other hand, the criteria of which basis objects were consciously chosen before reaching its final deposition context remain to be explored through the analysis of the same objects. In this way, funerary amulets can provide us with the understanding of information about funerary practices, faiths and symbolic beliefs that guided the ancient Egyptian mortuary customs and mind-set.

This paper focuses on the symbolism of the materials used in funerary amulets from the Egyptian collection of the Musée du Louvre. The project's main goal is to raise awareness of the materiality of the relationship between amulets and funerary rituals, such as mummification and the "opening of the mouth" ritual. Amulets played a role in these activities because they were supposed to protect the deceased in their way to the underworld. On this purpose, during the process of embalming, priests were responsible for the introduction of amulets between the mummies' bandages (Albert 2012, 81). If all types of amulets were suitable for the funerary purposes remains an open question. However, comparative studies of amulets on mummies indicate a certain consistency. The repetition of types, materials of manufacture and colours of funerary amulets is a common phenomenon.

Indeed, funerary amulets were selected according to their shape, but also their material and their colour. The Book of the Dead chapters (Barguet 1967) and other textual sources, such as pMacGregor (Capart, 1909) and the inscription in the Ptolemaic temple at Dendera (Cauville, 1997), provide a series of instructions regarding the material of amulets. However, it is possible to find some variations. Archaeology displays that the materialities of amulets are diverse: they are made of gold and silver, lapis lazuli, turquoise, carnelian, jasper, faience, etc. Their symbolism and meaning are also diverse, but far away from the pure chance. The material in what amulets were made defines their symbolism and apotropaic qualities because the use of the correct material guaranteed the puissance of amulets (Ikram and Dodson 1998, 137). Differences in materials could suggest variations depending on social context and religious beliefs or practices.

According to the Oxford English Dictionary, materiality is "the quality of being composed of matter". In the case of Egyptian amulets, this distinction in the symbolism of materials explains the differences uses of amulets, such as amulets made in gold were selected for burial because of their imperishable proprieties and others material more accessible, like Egyptian faience, were chosen for diary uses.

Therefore, the analysis of funerary amulets helps us to unveil which symbolic aspects laid behind the selection and use of certain materials and colours. In fact, the Egyptian word for "colour", iwen, also means "nature" or "character" (Wilkinson 1994, 104). For this reason, colour becomes an important way of adding life and individuality to an image or an artefact, such as amulets. In this manner, we have seen that the external appearance, given by the colour, was the essence of the artefact, that is, its own materiality. For instance, in my database of amulets from the collections of the Louvre, I have found amulets of vultures that are supposed to be in gold manufactured in electrum. However, their magical properties and their funerary purpose are still active because vultures have still golden appearance. In other words, as we see in the Shakespeare's *The Merchant of Venice*: "All that glitters is not gold".

What it is a funerary amulet?

The word "amulet" commonly means any small object that, due to its shape, material and colour, has magical properties to protect its owner (Petrie 1914, 1). Nevertheless, due to the variety of shapes and functions, defining what is an amulet is a complicated task. Firstly, one could assume that an amulet is a personal item because it was meant to be worn on the body (Klasens 1975, 222) to favour the transmission of its magical powers to its owner, which makes the defining criterion. Thus, in most cases, the size of amulets allows researchers to distinguish them from other objects of the funeral equipment, such as ex-votos due to their portable character in burials (Stevens 2006). However, the main quality of amulets is based on their function.

The amulet guarantees the luck of its owner by protecting them from misfortune in daily life. Because of this apotropaic feature, amulets were also carried by its owner in death, therefore extending its magical properties into the afterlife. Indeed, amulets were usually placed close to the body, usually between the mummy's bandages (Albert 2012, 81). The embalming of the mummy was a dangerous and uncertain stage, as the deceased has not yet integrated the underworld (Barbotin 2008, 44). This is the reason why the use of amulets in funerary rituals was an important matter for Egyptians.

As well as funerary practices, the materiality of amulets have changed across Egyptian history (Andrews 1994, 7). Amulets are well attested since the Early Dynastic Period but their number have remarkably increased from the New Kingdom onwards (Ikram and Dodson 1998, 142). Gradually, they trickled-down to the rest of society, which contributed to the diversification of materials used in amulets manufacture. In this manner, Petrie excavated Late Period mummies at Hawara that were embellished with a great number of amulets (Petrie 1914, 173).

As a matter of fact, what we mean by "symbolism" is of overwhelming importance to the Egyptian civilisation. So, we must consider that the choice of a specific amulet's shape was not left to chance. Given apart the aesthetic aspect and personal taste, amulets were chosen because of their magical powers. The same idea applies to the election of material and the manufacture's colour. These criteria were the base of the amulet's meaning, by providing it with magical powers and benefits, that were understood by the common people. According to Wilkinson, "the Egyptian concept of magic was also based on an idea of the implicit nature of things - the belief in a universal supernatural force that was the prerogative of the gods but available to humans through sympathetic means" (Wilkinson 1994, 7). In other words, amulets contribute to the maintenance of the Egyptian concept of harmony, *Maat*.

Materiality of Egyptian funerary amulets was a key aspect. In fact, Egyptian culture gave a lot of importance to the universal harmony, Maat, that is, the natural and cyclical evolution of events. We can distinguish it daily in the rise of the Nile when, after a period of drought, the long river covers the land and agriculture can start again. In the same manner, when a person died, he could rebirth in the afterlife, just as Osiris did. In the funerary field, Maat is the magical force that equalise the balance during the weighting of the heart (spell 125 of the Book of the Dead). To that extent, amulets were given to men like a certain manner of control this natural balance (Germond 2005, 13).

The materiality of Egyptian funerary amulets

Although it is quite obvious, I would like to remark that the Book of Going Forth by Day, commonly called the Book of the Dead, is the wealthiest written source of the Egyptian funerary field, largely employed since the New Kingdom. It is also the most useful one for researchers, who we can appreciate through its pages several difficult trials that the deceased must pass to obtain the eternal life. The deceased had to recite several formulas to face the funerary geniuses, protectors of the gates of the afterlife (Barbotin 2008, 23). To help him accomplish the task, since the New Kingdom, this group of papyrus accompanied the deceased in their grave, that is, they were also a personal funerary object. Actually, every book was put into the grave so it could be used even as another funerary amulet (Dodson and Ikram 1998, 138). Even if it is possible to establish similarities between them, each papyrus was personalised with the deceased's name, so they are unique.

In a similar manner, scholars must consider funerary amulets as a personal object too. In fact, most of them were carried during their owner's life, so they were engraved with the name of the deceased (obviously, most of the examples belong to the Pharaoh and his close relations). In other cases, some amulets were inscribed by a certain formula of the Book of the Dead (for the spells carved on the heart-scarabs, see Malaise, 1978).

On the contrary to the papyrus of the Book of the Dead, with its unique iconographic and writing style, amulets were mass-produced artefacts. In other words, archaeological discoveries display the same typology of amulets throughout the whole Egyptian territory. Materials chosen for funerary amulets were not due to a chance, because they are always submitted to a complex symbolical aspect. As a matter of fact, certain spells of the Book of the Dead express the obligation to create a funerary amulet in a precise material - e.g., the spell 155 suggests that the djed-pillar, as representation of Osiris and stability, should only be confectioned in gold due to the incorruptibility of this material (Albert 2012, 84).

Nevertheless, archaeological discoveries show us a great variety of funerary amulets and materials. In fact, "Pliny mentions about thirty different kinds of precious stones obtained from Egypt and Ethiopia, but relatively few of these can be identified" (Lucas and Harris 1962, 386). In the case of funerary amulets, comparative studies of their typology can be developed between the collections of different archaeological sites and museums, where they are currently preserved. Nevertheless, we can find differences in amulet's materials and its colours.

This is why the materiality of Egyptian amulets, that is to say, the material of which they were manufactured, is a trustworthy source for the study of the Egyptian culture. In fact, according to Germond (2005, 115), it is the material that transfers to the amulet all its power.

I would like to present a short list of the most employed materials in the manufacturing of amulets, based on other studies, but also on my database of the collections of the Musée du Louvre.

Gold, the flesh of the gods, is one of the most employed materials because of its connection with the sun and life (Yoyotte, 1987), but mostly because of its powerful imperishability (Aufrère 1997, 129). Ancient sources (e.g., Herodotus III, 114) mentioned that gold in particular could be found in a large amount in the mines of the oriental desert, but mainly in Nubia. It has been very much employed in the manufacture of amulets, but also in other artefacts being part of the funerary treasure, such as chests and masks. We must also notice that golden funerary artefacts have been found in graves since the Early Dynastic Period (Lucas and Harris 1962, 224). In this manner, I have collected amazing golden hearts (figure 1). In fact, the spell 30 of the Book of the Dead specifies that the heart scarab must be manufactured in gold, because the heart is necessary to accomplish the rebirth of the deceased. So, its extended use is due to its symbolism as daily renewal, but also to practical reasons like its accessibility.

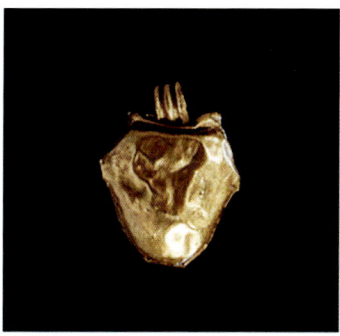

Figure 1: Heart amulet in gold, Musée du Louvre (AF 9101). © Musée du Louvre/Georges Poncet.

As for it, silver - the gods' bones - was related to the crescent moon, just like the goddess Hathor and the god Thot. However, it was an imported material, so most examples belong to the New Kingdom and afterwards (Wilkinson 1994, 84).

We can find the combination of golden and silver amulets, but also its variety, electrum, "the white gold". It was a material mostly used as substitute for gold. However, we cannot deny its importance, as for instance, the top of obelisks was covered with electrum (Lucas and Harris 1962, 235).

Iron, due to its meteoritic origin, had a particular significance (Wilkinson 1994, 85). It was related to the god Seth. Amulets made of iron were rare, except the headrest-shaped ones. However, most of artefacts employed during the "opening of the mouth" ritual were manufactured in this material (spell 149 of the Book of the Dead).

Together with metals, precious and semi-precious stones were also important materials used for the manufacture of amulets. Among them, I would like to remark the role of lapis lazuli and turquoise. Researchers argue if the first material came from Egypt or if it was mostly imported from Afghanistan (Germond 2005, 23). In any case, its symbolism was very important for Egyptian culture because the hair of the gods was made of this material. Both are a symbol of fecundity and rebirth, but also of the nocturne sky, obviously because of its colour (Wilkinson 1994, 88). They have been widely employed in the manufacture of amulets, but also of jewellery. A great number has been discovered in the royal tombs, as Tutankhamun's and the royal tombs at Tanis (Nicholson and Shaw 2000, 40; Yoyotte 1987, 232). Because of its blue colour and its symbolism, that is, the dynamism and rebirth, they have always been related to the goddess Hathor. In fact, I would like to note that she was referred as "the turquoise Goddess". I would also like to emphasise that, in Thebes, Hathor was the guardian of the necropolis and deceased.

Carnelian is one of the most employed symbols of life. It also represents the destructing forces of the desert, in relationship with the god Seth. It was in use since the Early Dynastic Period, because it is accessible in the desert between the Nile Valley and the Red Sea, normally in red or orange colour. It was a material very frequently employed by the Egyptians in the funerary equipment: of course, amulets, but also jewellery, scarabs and coffins' accessories (Nicholson and Shaw 2000, 27).

Jasper is found in a great variety of colours, such as red, green, brown, black and yellow. However, the most employed colour was green, a symbol of new vegetation, and red, a symbol of new life, colours used in manufacture of beads and amulets (Lucas and Harris 1962, 397).

I would like to point out that stones were an important source for amulets' manufacturing, because of their hardness and durability. Clearly, stones are very important in the history of religion due to their symbolism. In particular, Egyptian mythology express the world's creation though the Benben stone

(Wilkinson 1994, 88). Several other stones were employed, such as diorite, steatite, serpentine, amazonite, malachite, and obsidian

Due to their symbolism related to conceptions of rebirth, several amulets were manufactured in faience. Named as "the brilliant", because of its metallic luminosity, it is a typically Egyptian material which was used from the Early Dynastic Period until the Islamic Period. It is important to clarify the difference between glazed ceramic and faience. Whereas the first was a clay core covered by a glazed layer, the second one has a glazed material in its core (Mulford 1982, 26). We can find it in several colours, like green, white, black and yellow, but the most common was the blue, because of its relationship with the goddess Hathor. Its connection with the funerary realm is quite obvious, as materialised in the funerary servants (ushabtis) which were manufactured in blue faience. Mummies from Late and Greco-Roman periods were covered by a hairnet made of blue faience, for protecting them, on which funerary amulets were placed (Andrews 1994, 8).

Archaeological discoveries have displayed funerary amulets in others materials, like wood or wax (Raven 1983). However, although interesting due to their symbolism, I have not taken such amulets in consideration because they are less numerous in graves. I suppose that, due to their fragility, they were not acceptable for supporting the passage towards the afterlife.

I also would like to stress on the existence of written amulets, that is, papyrus inscribed with a funerary formula. They have been found between the mummies' bandages (Albert 2012, 81) and they operated in practice like two-dimensional amulets. However, due to their immense diversity, that is, their difficult classification, I have not included them in this paper.

The materiality of amulets is a diverse and rich source of study. I have also found amulets manufactured in two different materials - e.g., scarabs made of stone and glass, or papyrus' columns made of faience whose details were marked in gold. Funerary pectorals are another example of the combination of materials. However, I consider that all materials have not been acceptable for the manufacture of funerary amulets - e. g., alabaster was a typically Egyptian material, mostly employed in the manufacture of statues and vases. Nevertheless, in spite of the symbolism and the relationship with conceptions of rebirth, I have not found any amulet made of this material in the Musée du Louvre's collection.

According to Wilkinson, regarding materials, "the outward appearance was no more important than inner substance" (Wilkinson 1994, 82). In other words, the external vision was rather important for the Egyptians. Each colour was associated with a specific idea (Davies 2001, 158). In the case of amulets, if they were made of gold or electrum is due to the sources' accessibility or even the purchasing power of its owner. However, it is thanks to its external aspect that the funerary amulet owned a particular purpose.

The materiality of Egyptian colours

According to Wilkinson, who completed a study about the symbolism of Egyptian colours, "it seems sure that some connection usually existed in the minds of the Egyptians between a given sign and the colour used to depict it" (Wilkinson 1994, 111). Thus, the organisation of colours in ancient Egyptian art was not the result of pure chance. This is the reason why we find, in papyri or in wooden coffins, that amulets were always depicted in the same range of colours. Every sign was depicted in a precise colour because it had its own significance (Davies 2001, 158).

In the case of funerary amulets, as magical artefacts, they were provided with protective and apotropaic powers, with the aim of transferring them to the deceased. These properties derived from their material of which amulets were manufactured, but also their colours (Klasens 1975, 232).

Even if the Egyptian palette was actually very rich, we can distinguish six colours that are frequently repeated in funerary amulets:

The colour black was made from coals, it is the most characteristic funerary colour. Some divinities' amulets, like Anubis in his jackal form, were manufactured in black in direct relationship with the underworld. Maybe because black was also the colour of natron, employed during the mummification's process. However, black could also be the colour of the fertile land of the Nile Valley. In other words, quite the opposite to our contemporary way of thinking, in ancient Egypt black was used with funerary purposes because of its relationship with life, as a symbol of fertility and resurrection. In fact, "the symbolic association of the colour with life and fertility may well have originated in the fertile black silt deposited by the Nile River in its annual flooding" (Wilkinson 1994, 109). The two fingers amulet, placed on the incision made during the mummification process, was manufactured in black obsidian because of its rebirth power.

The famous "Egyptian blue" was the result of the combination between iron and copper oxides and quartz. Naturally, it was associated with the life-bringing waters of the Nile, that is, it was the symbol of life and fertility, birth and rebirth. It was also related to the sky. Maybe because of this, it was used as a symbol of protection. In fact, many amulets of the god Bes and Taweret were made of blue colour, because they protected women during the childbirth. Blue was also a very significant colour used for funerary artefacts, such as in the tombs' paintings. In our database from Louvre's collection, many wedjat amulets (figure 2), the stripped eye of the god Horus, were manufactured in these tonalities to contribute to the complete restore of the eye. In this fashion, amulets in falcon' shape, the animal representation of Horus, were also blue. The Four Sons of Horus, whose amulets were shaped as canopic jars, used for preserving the viscera of deceased in the afterlife. Their blue colour and their assembled position served as a guarantee for the deceased's rebirth.

Figure 2: Wedjat amulet in blue-green faïence, Musée du Louvre (E 16206). © Musée du Louvre/Georges Poncet.

Green, the colour of vegetation, was obtained from the malachite. We must consider the importance of vegetation because, in the middle of the desert, an oasis was a symbol of hope. This is the reason why green was the colour of growth, life, afterlife and resurrection. Almost all papyrus' column amulets were made in green colour. Because of its relationship with vitality but mostly regeneration, green was also used for the eye of Horus amulet.

White was obtained from calcium. It is the colour of purity by excellence, but also the symbol of clarity and sacredness. Consequently, objects used in rituals, such as vases and bowls, were manufactured in white alabaster. As far as the amulets are concerned, on the one hand, it was employed in the representation of some sacred animals, like the white cow. On the other hand, it was obviously the colour of the white crown's amulet, in opposition to the red crown and in relation with solar divinities.

Red was made from iron's oxides and ochre, it is the colour of both sun and blood. Because of this, it was a symbol of the vitality and energy, but it could also be the representation of danger and destruction—e.g. the god Seth, who murdered his brother Osiris and brought chaos to the world, was usually depicted with a red face. Because of its relation with blood, the basis of life, it was the colour chosen for the heart amulet and the heart scarab too, as the centre of the life itself. It was also the colour employed for the tyet amulet (figure 3), or girdle of Isis, made of red carnelian (spell 156 of the Book of the Dead). On the opposite, the head of serpent amulets was also made of red carnelian, with the aim of controlling it. The interpretation depends on the context, because the crown of Lower Egypt was also in red.

Figure 3: Girdle of Isis amulet in red carnelian, Musée du Louvre (E 2208). © Musée du Louvre/Georges Poncet.

Yellow was made from different oxides and ochre, it was obviously in relation with the sun, that is, a symbol of life and eternity. It was also the colour of the flesh of the gods, so it was in direct relation with gods and sacred images. As a matter of fact, priests carried yellow clothes during the funerary rituals (Wilkinson 1994, 108). Archaeological discoveries display a group of amulets manufactured in this colour, such as scarabs made of faience. We would like to focus on the golden amulets. This is a particular category whose economic importance cannot be denied. Even if gold was an accessible material in ancient Egypt, it was employed just for a group of amulets - e.g., in our database ureus amulets were made of gold, just as the spell 157 of the Book of the Dead commands. As well, most of pectorals were made of this material.

Nevertheless, I would like to remark that colour is not an absolute criterion. Ignoring the personal interpretations' factor, I have found several difficulties for distinguishing the colours of amulets - e.g., the difference between blue and green is not always so easy to establish. In fact, in my database, I had to create a special category for greenish blue or "blue-green" colour, because most of the amulets made of Egyptian faience display a colouring between blue and green. In this manner, the djed-pillar amulet, as a representation of the vertebral column of Osiris, as well as a symbol of stability, appears in blue-green.

Both materials and colours were a symbol of life and vitality, so the difference for Egyptians had a limited significance.

Thus, I also would like to notice the differences in the intensity of colours. In particular, amulets made of faience present a very characteristic aspect that lay out from azure blue to turquoise. I ignored if the change in their coloration was deliberate or, on the contrary, they it was a matter of chance during the manufacture process.

In addition, archaeological discoveries have displayed the combination of colours. On the one hand, there are amulets actually manufactured in orange, brown or beige colours. In fact, we must consider that it was the combination of several elements found in nature that created different colours. In practice, craftsmen repeated the same recipe, so finally, colours were standardised. In this way, all Egyptian statues and walled paintings display the difference between men, with dark skin, and women, with lighter skin. On the other hand, there were amulets whose details were painted in another tonality.

We must also consider the fact that colours deteriorate (Davies, 2001). In fact, the Egyptian palette has not been modified until the Roman Period. However, a closer inspection reveals that some colours are currently changed or lost. As we have seen, Egyptian colours are composed by mineral pigments and synthetic colorants, which have changed since their application. In my research, I have noticed variations in bluish amulets, which have turned in black. The same idea can be applied for metallic amulets, whose current greenish aspect is a product of oxidation.

The external aspect of amulets is a remarkable feature to be considered. However, it cannot be the defining criterion in the interpretation of such objects. We must pay attention to their manufacture and symbolic aspects, but also the evolution of their materiality in Egyptian history. In other words, the knowledge of Egyptian colours and their symbolism is fundamental in the understanding of funerary amulets.

Conclusions

In spite of the minuscule size of amulets, the analysis of their materiality and symbolism turns them into a very rich source of study. Within the study of amulets, I would like to distinguish the figure of William Mathew Flinders Petrie, one of the most productive British Egyptologists, whose pioneering work was focused on the relationship between funerary amulets and mummification. He was, indeed, the first to establish a corpus of funerary amulets placed on mummies from the Late Period, by paying attention to archaeological context. According to Petrie, "the whole subject of amulets is an immense one, and there is no general work of reference giving the ideas of various lands" (Petrie 1914, 4).

Considered as jewellery, amulets have continued to be a protective item. Magical powers were really incorporated in their materiality. In spite of their trivial size, they are the evidence of Egyptians' search for perfection, looking forward to re-establishing the universal harmony, Maat. Due to the refinement in their manufacture, amulets have surpassed the category of adornment for being promoted to masterpieces.

As part of the ancient art, Egyptian handwriting was composed by sacred images, mostly understood by priests, so common people had to find their own way to take part in religion and the funerary process. We must not ignore that death was conceived as a continuation of life. However, Egyptian inscriptions reflect the concern of death presented like a final and perpetual separation from life. Popular texts such as the Harper's Song reveal that "no one who has gone returns" (Barbotin 2008, 21). In fact, the path to reach afterlife was full of dangers and trials. If the deceased do not surpass it, they will not revive in the netherworld. This is the reason why Egyptians paid so much attention to the correct development of the funerary process.

Pharaohs and nobles were buried in a rich tomb furnished with wall paintings and sumptuous funerary objects, including several types of amulets. Actually, Tutankhamen's grave is one of the most extraordinary examples. The pharaoh was protected by more than 140 amulets, mostly made in gold (Ikram and Dodson 1998, 137). Due to its non-plundered condition, it is a unique source for researchers.

Nevertheless, ordinary people did not have access to a such a burial. In this matter, Herodotus made a complete description of three different types of mummification made during the Late Period, which depended on the deceased's wealth. Apparently, economic capacities were also a determining factor of an amulet's materiality. Obviously, rich people could afford funerary amulets close to the Book of the Dead's prescriptions. In other words, they could buy golden amulets. On the contrary, unfortunate people could afford only gold-coloured amulets, that is, manufactured in electrum or even in yellow faience. Actually, materials could be imitated thanks to a glazed or even painted cover. Thus, the importance of colours over material, as centre of the underlying symbolism of amulets, is clear.

Actually, studying the Egyptian symbolism becomes a difficult task due to its pluralism. On the one hand, different amulets could have several meanings depending on their context. On the other hand, materiality studies also afford us to determine the amulet's dating - e.g., the yellow jasper was not used in the manufacture of jewellery before the Roman Period (Nicholson and Shaw 2000, 30), whereas turquoise has been in use continuously since the Early Dynastic Period (Nicholson and Shaw 2000, 62).

There are also practical reasons to which we have to pay attention in materiality studies. According to Nicholson and Shaw, most scarab amulets were made of stone rather than faience, maybe because of an easier lecture of hieroglyphic symbols (Nicholson and Shaw 2000, 181).

In this sense, we have to admit that the difference between funeral and daily amulets is difficult to establish, given the fact that amulets are personal items and most of them were supposed to be carried by their owner during their lifetime (Klasens 1975, 233). However, the materiality of amulets provides us some with keys, because funerary amulets were specifically created for graves. For this purpose, the study of materials and colours is not pejorative. It is the case for the sacred cow made of gold, who have to be placed in the deceased's neck (spell 162 of the Book of the Dead), on the opposite to other cow amulets used daily for obtaining the protection of the goddess Hathor.

In conclusion, amulets were supposed to guarantee the deceased's passage towards the afterlife, but also his eternal destination. Due to the dangers of this path, the future Osiris had to be protected and well equipped. In this sense, funerary amulets were the weapons of the deceased to confront the demons that reside in the underworld. The shape of amulets was not enough to accomplish all the trials, so their magical powers were increased by their material and colour. In other words, the symbolism of materiality in funerary amulets was essential in the Egyptian culture. Through their study we can understand the stability of the green Osiris' column, the revitalised blood of the red Isis' knot and the regenerative force of the blue Horus' eye. Just like the deceased, the Egyptian funerary amulets are currently presented in museums as the materiality of eternity.

References

Albert, F. 2012. Amulets and funerary manuscripts. In M. Müller-Roth and M. Höveler-Müller eds. **Grenzen Des Totenbuchs. Ägyptische Papyri Zwischen Grab Und Ritual/Beyond the Book of the Dead. Egyptian Papyri between Tomb and Ritual**. Rahden: Verlag Marie Leidorf, 71–86.

Andrews, C. 1994 **Amulets of Ancient Egypt**. London: British Museum Press.

Aufrère, S. 1997. L'Univers minéral dans la pensée égyptienne: essai de synthèse et perspectives. **Archéo-Nil** 7, 113–144.

Barbotin, C. ; Dunand, F. and Gasse, A. 2008. **La Momie Aux Amulettes. Catalogue de l'exposition du musée des Beaux-Arts et d'Archéologie**. Besançon: Musée des Beaux-Arts de Besançon.

Barguet, P. 1967. **Le Livre des morts des anciens Egyptiens**. Paris: Les éditions du cerf.

Capart, J. 1909. Une liste d'amulettes. **Zeitschrift für Ägyptische Sprache und Altertumskunde** 45, 14–21.

Cauville, S. 1997. **Le temple de Dendara. Les chapelles osiriennes**. Cairo: Institut Français d'Archéologie Orientale.

Davies, W. 2001. **Colour and Painting in Ancient Egypt**. London: The British Museum Press.

Dodson, A. and Ikram S. 1998. **The Mummy in Ancient Egypt. Equipping the dead for eternity**. London: Thames & Hudson, 137–146.

Etienne, M. 2009. **Les Portes Du Ciel. Visions Du Monde dans l'Egypte Ancienne**. Paris: Musée du Louvre Éditions.

Germond, P. 2005. **Le Monde Symbolique des Amulettes Égyptiennes**. Milan: 5 Continents.

Klasens, A. 1975. Amulet. **Lexikon der Ägyptologie**, Vol. 1, 232–236.

Lucas, A and Harris, J. 1962. **Ancient Egyptian Materials and Industries**. London: Histories & Mysteries of Man.

Malaise, M. 1978. **Les scarabées de coeur dans l'Egypte ancienne, avec un appendice sur les scarabées de coeur des Musées Royaux d'Art et d'Histoire de Bruxelles**. Brussels: Fondation égyptologique Reine Élisabeth.

Mulford, M., 1982. Egyptian Faience: Glazed Siliceous Ware. A Literature Survey. **AICCM Bulletin** 8, 26-32.

Nicholson, P. T. and I. Shaw. 2000. **Ancient Egyptian Materials and Technology**. Cambridge: Cambridge University Press.

Raven, M. 1983. Wax in Egyptian Magic and Symbolism. **Oudheidkundige Mededelingen uit het Rijksmuseum van Oudheden te Leiden** 64, 7–47.

Sauneron, S. 1952. **Rituel de l'embaumement**. Cairo: Service des Antiquités de l'Égypte.

Petrie, W.M.F. 1914. **Amulets**. London: Constable & Company.

Stevens, A. 2006. **Private Religion at Amarna: the Material Evidence**. Oxford: Archaeopress.

Wilkinson, R. H. 1994. **Symbol and Magic in Egyptian Art**. London: Thames and Hudson.

Yoyotte, J. 1987. **Tanis. L'or des pharaons**. Paris: Association française d'action artistique.

Materiality and history: some reflections

Marcelo Rede

The relations between historical studies and materiality oscillate from precariousness to rejection. The schism between them is ancient, deep-seated, and difficult to overcome. In general, historians despised or failed to consider the connections between social life and materiality. Notwithstanding their great diversity, rarely do theories of historical experience recognise the importance of the material dimension of human existence. Historiography was timid or totally inept in incorporating material sources in its knowledge generating process. Since its origins and due to a strongly entrenched vocation, historiography opted to privilege written sources of all types, granting material culture an illustrative role or a secondary place as corroboration of the contents of textual sources. It is worth adding that in reverse the situation is not much better. In many areas such as archaeology and art history, as well as anthropology and technology studies, analyses centred on material culture focused too much or even exclusively on the physical attributes of objects, their technical or aesthetic characteristics. Fundamental dimensions of the historiographical approach have been neglected, such as social context and temporal dynamics. The results were occasionally very useful in relation to forms and styles, materials and techniques, typologies and seriations, but frequently disappointing in terms a historical comprehension of societies.

Problems can thus be found in the ontological level about the nature of societies, as well as in the epistemological level regarding the conditions for constructing historical knowledge about past societies. Both deficiencies are intimately linked, and confronting them implies a dual effort: the reconsideration of ideas about the materiality of the social and, equally, the proposition of approaches that permit the definitive integration of material culture into the heuristic operation of historiography.

Among the social sciences, there have been many attempts to mobilise the physical realities (from artefacts to landscapes, and bodies to urban structures) for the production of knowledge. Significantly, the principal efforts occurred at the margins of historiography, and were more fruitful in anthropology, sociology, or even in philosophical reflections of nature, and the connections between the human and non-human.

The nineteenth century was marked by a sharpened sensitivity towards the material ingredients of the social trajectory (which was equally valid for the biological life of the species, as shown by the first steps in the theory of evolution by Darwin and others). On the one hand, the Industrial Revolution confronted part of Europe with an unprecedented volume of goods, turned into commodities bearing the marks of a fabulous technological process, since they circulated in an internally consolidated market in global expansion, and also because they were part of a circuit of discarding, replacing, and overcoming innovation that had never been seen at such a speed, and finally, because they represented the materialisation of a socially valued ideal of progress. It is difficult to conceive such a new world without taking into account ideas such as those of Marx, which addressed the impact, and eventually the malaise, generated by the spectacle of production, circulation, and consumption. On the other hand, colonisation placed Europeans in a position of continuous contact with distant peoples, e.g. Africans, Asians, and the peoples of Oceania. The emergent anthropology, which closely followed and even was part of the expansion process, was responsible for the intellectual effort of inserting these societies, seen as 'primitive' into an evolutionary line that tended to be universalising and placed Europe at the peak of civilisation. The great flow of objects—axes, canoes, totems, vessels, necklaces, bows, plumages etc.—

which formed and enriched the collections of the European centres, served as material basis for scholarly interpretation. Objects decisively became evidence of social formations, and their positioning on a scale was considered to be scientific. They offered tangible proofs for many of the current propositions of contemporary cultural theory, e.g. Henry Lewis Morgan and Edward Tylor.

The expansion of the explanatory potential of objects is well known. In previous centuries, the cabinets of curiosities were driven by the search for the extraordinary, for what broke with conventional categories through the 'exoticness', singularity, or distance from the 'normal' world. In nineteenth century ethnographic collections the logic of taxonomy prevailed, the establishment of standards that would give a concrete expression to ideas about the social organisation of peoples under the observation of European scholars. An acute scientism guided the whole effort and inspired the natural sciences, already well advanced in terms of verifiable criteria of knowledge. One of the institutional consequences of this logic was the fact that ethnographic collections were housed in natural history museums. This is how geology's stratigraphy, or the mutations of fossils in biology, the stylistic studies of technology etc. offered the organising principles of ethnographic collections, archaeological excavations, studies of 'primitive art,' and, more generally, for the social sciences (Buchli, 2004a, 180; Hicks 2010, 30s).

However, the ethnographic collectionism, which marked the formation of anthropology, did not last as the guiding principle of the new discipline. Here the first important schism occurred, which has been already verified in historiography. In history, the choice of literate societies as a zone of interest and, consequently, the affirmation of the privileged status of the written document, prolonged a secular inheritance from the biblical exegesis and the erudition of Greco-Latin textual studies. A division of labour was imposed, with the result that societies without writing migrated into the orbit of archaeologists and pre-historians. In anthropology, the initial tendency—which had found its framework with Pitt Rivers (his works were heavily supported by the empirical studies of objects and his ethnographic collection became the eponymous Museum in Oxford University in 1884)—gave way to an era of monographs about the social organisation of human groups. The study of objects was gradually marginalised and circumscribed to the universe of museums, where there prevailed the logic of collection, classification, and analyses whose scope consisted of the artefacts themselves. Artefacts which in exhibitions continued to fulfil their function of making visible and tangible the programmatic spectacle in which Europe and, subsequently, the US reinforced the superiority of its civilised identity, heirs of the Greco-Roman civilisations. Similarly, the field of folklore was for much of the twentieth century a refuge for studies of material culture, especially popular culture. Generally speaking, its pretension only rarely exceeded the limits of empirical properties of artefacts to historical analyses of everyday life.

In the initial decades of the twentieth century, Bronislaw Malinowski, Alfred Radcliffe-Brow, Franz Boas, and a large part of Anglo-Saxon anthropology, privileged fieldwork and consecrated themes such as religious or ritual forms, economic or symbolic exchanges, and institutional organisation, not to speak of myth and kinship, which would quickly become the driving problems of the discipline. The displacement was broad and coincided roughly with the move from a diffusionist perspective (in which the identification of origin and the monitoring of the migration of techniques through the analysis of objects were central) to the functionalist approach (which emphasised the social behaviour captured by 'participant observation' without much intermediation of material documents). Afterwards, the great influence of the French anthropology of Émile Durkheim and Marcel Mauss imposed a largely abstract, institutional, and relational conception of the social fact. Consequently, during the first half of the twentieth century, material culture remained on the margins of the prevailing pathways in the social sciences.

As expected, material things remained at the centre of archaeology. However, here the situation varied. A dominating and traditional strand extended the object-centred view. Its main contribution was to establish the relations between archaeological materials and the cultural profiles to which they belonged, adjusting the chronology and the spatial distribution of what was discovered. This archaeology still had little impact on the interpretation of the social system and its mutations. There were, however, alternative efforts: for example, the 1930s and 1940s saw the emergence of V. Gordon Childe's theories on the 'agricultural and urban revolutions' which made use of evolutionism and diffusionism, with Marxist influences, to explain the Neolithic transition process and the emergence of complex societies in the Ancient Near East. Even Childe's approach remains an exception within the archaeology of the epoch, it is with no doubt the greatest example of analytical effort towards material culture.

In the 1960's the New Archaeology rebelled against everything associated with a descriptive and classificatory modus operandi. For the new archaeologists the equation between typologies of objects and cultures or 'peoples' appeared simplistic and insufficient. Their ambition was wider in the sense of considering archaeology not only a technique for obtaining information, but also a true social science, whose efforts had to explain the transformation processes of societies, hence the designation Processual Archaeology. Special attention was paid to the connections between society and the environment and the role of culture, including material culture as an adaptation mechanism. In a 1962 article entitled 'Archaeology as anthropology,' Lewis R. Binford, the patron of the new school, stated the intimate relationship between the two fields. It was in anthropology (particularly a cultural anthropology based on Leslie White) that archaeologists needed to seek the theoretical tools for building explanation (Watson, Leblanc and Redman 1971).

The advent of New Archaeology had the effect of a resounding paradigm shift, potentialised by the strong evangelising feature of its proponents. It also provoked reactions as relevant as the impact, both favourable and critical. For material culture studies and history, the first implication provoked by New Archaeology is probably a positive and practically unprecedented achievement with regard to the formation of the document. Singular objects and the site as a whole were usually interpreted as statistical data, without any consistent reflection on the process which had transformed them from live realities, functioning in a social context, to an archaeological deposit. New Archaeology introduced a fundamental concern with the composition of the material record. Reflections on the trajectory of artefacts and structures towards the formation of the archaeological record (Schiffer 1987) were supported by the ethnographic observation of the utilisation of material elements (inclusively disposal patterns) in living societies. Similarly, laboratory experiments aimed at verifying the physical behaviour of materials, processes of decomposition and preservation, which allowed a fine-tuning of the understanding of the residual universe that the researcher had under their eyes. It was thus sought not only to better understand the heuristic field of the discipline, but also to provide a more solid basis for the explanatory reasoning that assumed a shift in the attention of the archaeological site as a documentary locus to settlement as a sociological locus of human activity (David and Kramer 2001). This is a postulate which can be generalised, with obvious gains for the entire field of material culture studies.

In relation to history, to a certain extent, New Archaeology reacted to a traditional perspective which privileged 'civilizational' configurations and chronological successions, as opposed to an emphasis on the cultural system. New Archaeology also sought a holistic appreciation of societies and gave importance to the mechanisms of interaction between humans and the environment. In opposition to a merely descriptive narrative which privileged idiosyncratic events from documentary inductions (which New Archaeology identified as a mark of historiography, not without some militant exaggerations), the new archaeologists proposed an analytical procedure, largely based on the deductive models of the social sciences, inspired in turn by the natural sciences. Two collateral effects should be noticed by the historian: in the first place, the weakening of a diachronic perception, the reduction of the capacity to perceive and explain the dynamics of social mutation to the benefit of a more systemic and structural view, which allowed even the characterisation of Processual Archaeology as anti-historical. The second problem is the marginalisation of the ideological dimensions of reality, or symbolic systems. The lack of importance given by the first generation of new archaeologists to social representations in general would prove to be essential to the understanding of the developments of New Archaeology and the new trends in the study of material culture.

Signs of a profound shift in the consideration of material culture had accumulated since the late 1960s and stemmed from the combined influences of Lévi-Strauss's structuralism and Ferdinand de Saussure's linguistic-based semiology. French authors were precursors of the movement. Despite many differences, the works of Jean Baudrillard (Le système des objets, 1968) and Abraham Moles (Théorie des objets, 1972) shared the intention of describing the role of material things in modern consumer society and, above all, the appreciation of the symbolic function of objects. In this perspective, material culture is equated with a system of communication, through which societies create and express discursive contents, similar to what occurs with verbal codes. The analytical tools of linguistics are thus considered the best equippiment to unravel their meaning. Meanings that now present themselves as the true object of study, regardless of whether their support is material, iconographic, or verbal. Thus, the same pansemiotism that positively raised the problem of meaning in the humanities contributed for diluting the specificities of the various discursive mechanisms under an intended homogeneity of a general grammar.

The two elements above—the focus on more contemporary societies and the semiotic approach—have also penetrated archaeology. To cite a pioneer, James Deetz's work on the material culture of the North American colonial past (In small things forgotten: an archaeology of early American life, 1977) not only sought to reconstitute worldviews of the community from artefacts that had merited the attention of traditional classics and scholarship in the decorative arts and vernacular architecture only for classificatory and non-interpretive attention, but also encouraged archaeologists to explore chronological and societal profiles previously reserved for historians who had limited themselves to written documentation. The way was thus opened for the consolidation of historical archaeology, which allowed the overcoming of some entrenched but unproductive dichotomies. The study of modern and contemporary societies could also benefit, in the same way as prehistoric groups or ancient civilisations, from the analysis of material culture (cf. Orser and Fagan 1995).

It is no exaggeration to say that in the 1970's, material culture was brought to the attention of various fields, from American studies to the sociology of consumption, amalgamating tendencies that contemplated the growing interest in everyday relationships, the sharing of less erudite or formalised values and behaviour of the lower layers of social scale (Harvey 2010, 3). Evidence that concerns material culture were not confined to the tribes of anthropologists or to the disappeared societies of archaeologists. The consolidation of a mass consumer society after World War II had already encouraged scholars to consider the universe of material things, particularly in their commodity form. Now the concern with the symbolic meanings of consumption is what is presented to some extent as a novelty.

Another change was the shift in focus from the productive process and circulation—until then the centre of attention of economics and sociology, both classic and Marxist—to consumption, understood not only as the final act within a productive chain, dedicated to meeting needs, but also a moment for the reception of messages and the expression of values in a communication system. Mary Douglas and

Baron Isherwood in their equally pioneering work of 1979, precisely sought to make advances in relation to aspects of consumption that had remained obscure in traditional sociological theories (in spite of Thorstein Veblen's early and instigating propositions about conspicuous expenditure as a marker of class, dating from 1899), such as the ways of constructing personality and social identity through the consumption of goods or even ritual aspects which, far from being confined to so-called 'primitive' societies, enabled the modern consumer to position themself in an unchecked and emotionally destabilising capitalist system for the movement of goods (Douglas and Isherwood 1996)

The consideration of consumption as a social act creating meaning strongly marked the anthropology of consumption in the 1980s and 1990s, reinforcing the semiological dimension of studies of material culture of modern and contemporary societies. In the view of one of its main exponents, Daniel Miller, consumption is a phenomenon of interpretation, generation, and the appropriation of meanings through the mobilisation of goods in a market with a wide-ranging scale; a phenomenon of masses, which is not limited to the preferences, tastes and choices of an elite; a phenomenon that is no longer regarded with the mistrust of some previous economists, who considered it as the basis of the process of alienation; a phenomenon to be treated in its creative and positive nature (Miller 1987).

Similarly, in the field of social psychology, the roles of material culture in the social production of the individual were insisted upon. Even as an element of stabilisation from the self, since by definition material culture is endowed with a relatively fixed and lasting physicality, capable of guaranteeing constancy of relations: in the light of the psychic dependence of goods and the need to anchor the personality through acquisition, possession, use, disposal, exhibition etc., the study of interactions between the individual and society through material culture allows access to important phenomena, usually neglected by the social sciences (Csikszentmihalyi 1993). One aspect that needs to be emphasised is the tendency to go beyond a more restrictive view, but one with a long course in the psychological discipline, which tends to encapsulate the problems mentioned above in the sphere of the individual. What is increasingly seen is, to the contrary, a questioning of the social connections which configure individual expression and, at the same time, the mechanisms by which individuals construct images of self-definition from external references, including material ones (Dittmar 1992).

In parallel, the reaction to New Archaeology or Processual Archaeology was also characterised by the influence of linguistically oriented approaches and by a focus on the universe of meanings. More than an element of adaptation in relation to the environment, with mainly technical and economic functionalities, material culture began to be considered as a priority because of its potential to create and communicate meaning. In other words, through its discursiveness. However, other elements have made contributions: in the early 1980s, Ian Hodder—an author who would later play a great role as a theorist of Post-Processual Archaeology—sensed the excessively static limits of structuralist models for the analysis of historical dynamics. This led the new approach to seek in authors such as Pierre Bourdieu and Anthony Giddens a theory of social practice that could give individuals the performance capacities for acting and more active interactions with established structures, as well as an approximation with the historiography of the Annales, which began to give greater prominence to the studies of representational phenomena (Hodder 1982). Nevertheless, the analogy between material culture and texts and its implications in the methodological level prevailed: the use of the tools of linguistics and semiotics for the 'reading' of material elements. Hereafter, material culture was seen as a language whose code had to be deciphered. The textual metaphor largely prevailed in the later variations of studies of material culture, whether in archaeology (cf. Tilley 1990), or in anthropology (cf. Miller 1998).

Moreover, under the influence of hermeneutics and phenomenology, and authors such as Derrida and Foucault, explanation, based on objective scientific models, gave way to interpretation, a more fluid notion that allowed multifocal approaches, contemplating differentiated perceptions. As a result, from an ideological and even political point of view, the imposition of a single view of science was questioned as too unequivocal and too Eurocentric. Similarly, the belief that objective data could be compared to verify the validity of explanatory hypotheses, something which had guided Processual Archaeology, was seriously called into question by the Post-Processualists' conviction that the material record was sufficiently ambiguous and that its perception depends on subjective and cultural variants. In a cognitive process in which the elements of understanding an object are constructed, an object thus stops being considered as inert data in order to be seen as result of interventions by a subject—similarly to the meanings created by readers in dynamic interactions with texts. This was not an isolated case, but the irremediable connection of various disciplines with the intellectual environment influenced by the linguistic turn, especially since the 1980's. The criticism which gave rise to this perspective will be returned to in the second part of this chapter.

Despite being predominant, the consideration of material culture as having a discursive nature and the concern with symbolic phenomena were not exclusive, and it is worth mentioning a French perspective that sought to recover aspects of the materiality of things, particularly in their relation to the corporeality of human agents. Jean-Pierre Warnier (Warnier 1999) proposed returning to a suggestion of Marcel Mauss that, undeservedly, had had little repercussion in French anthropology. In a 1936 text in the Journal of Psychology, Mauss sought to lay the groundwork for an analysis of body habits and postures. Although Mauss intended to distance himself from traditional approaches to archaeology and technology studies, centred on techniques of instrument use, and preferred to emphasise 'body techniques', Warnier considers the dichotomy to be more pedagogical than ontological, and that Mauss' efforts had laid the groundwork for an examination of social practices based on the connections between the body and material culture. This did not involve focusing only on situations in which the body directly manipulated physical realities, but also inserting in the field of observation relations that are less noticeable in everyday life, such as the spatial arrangement of elements in the environment the body inhabits. The notion of motricity thus insists on the fact that the corporal conduct does not take place in a vacuum, but in terms of material parameters, which offer possibilities and impose limits. Moreover, in the conception defended by Warnier, it is not a question of analysing two distinct poles, which are defined by the exteriority of one in relation to the other: to the contrary, the material universe can be considered part of its own corporeality in a synthesis that, far from being static, implies dynamic interaction between body, space, and objects.

Hence, the focus of analysis is the process of incorporation, understood as the appropriation of the physical universe mediated by the body: a multiple appropriation which emerges in psychic, social and biological dimensions. In addition, in Mauss' conception as adopted by Warnier, it is the subject who operates the connections: if society establishes the reference schemes for the individual to position himself before the collective, individual psychology provides the mechanisms of interaction between the corporal subject and society. For scholars, what is most interesting is the singular way in which the subject appropriates the different variants and reproduces existence in their own manner. One can recognise here a departure from all forms of determinism (present in several versions of Marxism) and also from the postulate of a homology between structures (as in Pierre Bourdieu's concept of habitus). It is also recognisable a attempt to create a distance from the lineage of French anthropology from Durkheim to Lévi-Strauss, who had prioritised shared representations to the detriment of other dimensions of social action. Being attentive to the practices exercised by the body and being based on the materiality of the objects would therefore allow, if not an overcoming, at least a complementation of discursive analyses.

It is difficult to assess the approaches to material culture in historiography. Contacts have been sporadic and fragmentary. Nothing equivalent to the archaeological or anthropological debates has occurred among historians. Let us take a case that may be illustrative of the situation of precariousness: the Annales School. Not because it is representative of the entire discipline—which would be a rather erroneous judgment, somewhat stimulated by its widespread diffusion around the world—but since the Annales was a hotbed of methodological experiments and intense theoretical discussions, it would be expected that, among its followers, material culture would have been seriously considered as an element of the historiographical operation. Nothing, however, would be more false, and the examples that can be evoked reinforce this unease. Obviously, no one forgets Fernand Braudel's contributions in his monumental 1979 work Civilisation Matérielle, économie et capitalisme, in which there is a decisive insertion in the horizons of a socio-economic history of the palpable dimension of the goods that compose it. However, above all, this involves a thematic incorporation of the attention that emphasises the material elements behind the abstract notions of capitalism, commodity, circulation, etc., without implying an analysis of material culture itself, and without making it a documentary source with the right to full citizenship. In 1978, the collective work organised by Le Goff, Chartier and Revel, and which at times serves as a group manifesto, Jean-Marie Pesez's chapter on material culture, limits itself to argue for an enlargement of documentary corpora by the inclusion of material culture and the new possibilities that would be opened with this, but without providing any more guidance for more consistent treatment, or any reflection about the resulting theoretical implications or methodological needs. It seems to rely quite simply on the more or less generic transposition of archaeological procedures to the historiographical field (Pesez 1978).

In the following years, many works, generic or more monographic, indicated that Nouvelle Histoire's appeal for a renewal of themes, including material culture, had been met, though without a profound reformulation of the historian's analytical arsenal being necessary. Daniel Roche's book on the emergence of modern forms of consumption is very characteristic of this: a strong attention is given to the universe of material things and its role in the game of new sociabilities which emerged in modern times (something already well explored by the work of Michel de Certeau) coexists with a traditional methodology, based mainly on written documentation (Roche 1997). In another well-known case, the inclusion of a particular kind of material segment, the iconographic, through the work of Michel Vovelle, was oriented, first of all, by the expansion of the list of sources considered of greater potential to approach the mentalities and other related themes, such as the visions of death, the same logic which, in fact, led him to rely heavily on notary records (Vovelle 1974). The impact of the renewal of the thematic repertoire suggested by Vovelle—and accompanied by many of his colleagues in the Annales—is limited, however, by the reproduction of a semiotic method that contributed little to the renewal of iconographic analysis in the historiographic field, even if another point emphasised by Vovelle can be considered an advance, i.e. serial treatment.

Here New French History did not differ much from the general situation of historiography: little commitment to reflecting on the material dimensions of social organisation and timidity in relation to the insertion of material culture in the historiographical operation.

A fundamental problem in assessing the possibilities of relation between history and material culture rests on the actual appreciation of the material dimension of social reality. How does the material existence of this set of actions and relations we call society occur? Somewhat paradoxically, the physical nature of human phenomena is so ubiquitous and imposing that we tend to neglect it as an obvious fact. However, starting with the corporal constitution itself—of this body which is the first physical level to be dealt with and which people are conscious of—passing through the landscape, natural and artificial, and the plethora of objects. Instruments, machines, and so on, the totality of human action is endowed with a physical dimension. In other words, materiality underlies biological, psychic, and social life.

Trivialisation of this physicality brings with it, however, the risk of it being disregarded in the cognitive level. Aimed at dealing with social relations, human actions, and abstract phenomena (even if they are related to the most palpable concreteness), the social sciences reverberated, each in their own way, the tendency to dematerialise their objects.

The problem is embedded in the long tradition in Western thought in general, not only of a dualism between materiality and immateriality (manifested differently: material versus ideal, matter versus mind, sensory versus abstract, and so on), but also of a hierarchy that gives superior status to the second term of the equation, to the detriment of the former, with important repercussions in the way we perceive the world (Prown 1982, 2). In fact, to a large extent the triumphant march of the linguistic turn in the final decades of the twentieth century and its manifestations in the field of symbolic anthropology, Post-Processual Archaeology and multiculturalism in general—with its emphasis on discourse, representational meanings, and phenomena, and its focus on linguistic analytical tools and subjective interpretation—planted deep roots in idealist thought (Boivin 2008, 13). Precedence is conferred to thought, which, in turn, is conceived as an instance in which behaviour is generated; only from then on interaction with the material world starts to be taken into consideration, situated in the end of the chain: thought-behaviour-matter. Cartesian dualism and some of its implications are thus reproduced by conceptually separating the mind, thought, and language and, on the other hand, the body, practice, and material (Knappett 2005, 3; 6).

Another parallel aspect to be noticed is the centrality of the human. It may seem natural that in the social sciences the human occupies a place that is not only axial, but also one that orders, in the sense of establishing the subordination and the peripheral position of other elements. It is, however, an anthropocentrism artificially constructed by the subject of the act of knowledge and not by a condition inscribed in reality itself. Moreover, the 'human' we are talking about is an abstract, conceptual entity, set apart from its own materiality, even corporeal, and set aside and above the animal world within which it should be considered. It is a supraorganic and supramaterial human, based on which theoretical notions of society and culture have been constructed, as well as their necessary counterpoints: the animal, the material, the natural (Boivin 2008, 15).

Overcoming this situation is the main and most recent frontier in the debate on material culture, and has been particularly intense since the final years of the twentieth century. The movement of reaction is widespread, because it is a question of, faced with social sciences that are too humanised, recovering the biological and ecological dimensions of human, and in relation to what we are most interested in here, reconsidering the social in its interaction with materiality. Opposed to the empire of the 'linguistic turn', is thus a 'material turn'. In several domains, culturalism has tended to dematerialise objects (also understood as objects of study), and has been confronted by appeals in the sense of a rematerialisation of realities, the formulation of object-oriented theories, the valuation of nonhuman actors, whether they are animals or materials, overcoming the opposition between things and relations. In short, the incorporation of material sources in the process of knowledge (cf. Hicks and Beaudry 2010, 3). By extension, it has been advocated by approaches which have gone beyond the textual analogy to an understanding of the role of material things, not only because of the intrinsic methodological limitations that a semiology of linguistic origin presents when applied to material culture (or images), but also because, ontologically, this conception places the process of signification in an autonomous cultural site, disembodied from the (physical and imaginary) elements that vectorise the senses. Therefore, the idea that interaction with the physical universe is secondary is attacked, an act that only a concretised communication formulated in a purely mental instance, in which meanings were culturally condoned (Olsen 2003, 88).

It can be seen that, based on all the difficulties, there is recurrent schism between, on the one hand, culture or society and, on the other, the material. Furthermore, it can be seen that an entire tradition has located the active principle, the generator of human action, in a highly mentalised sphere of cultural patterns or largely abstract social interactions. Material culture has thus been reduced to passivity: not being endowed with the capacity of action alone, it is only the physically fulfilled reflection of the impulses of a matrix that precedes and is external to it. For example, if we return to the problem of meaning, we can reencounter the opposition between the conceptual representation of meaning, the attribute of an immanent human intelligence, and the resulting material manifestations of the signifier. The precedence and ascendancy of the mental over the natural can only be overcome if we accept that the conceptual formulation itself (of values, meanings, etc.) occurs in the interaction with materiality and that in a framework of complex relationships, capacities are not exclusively limited to human actors. In addition, things are endowed with vitality, they also exert motive power and act socially, shaping a framework of references, possibilities and limits to the human agent, whether they are aware of this or not. Far from being passively structured by man, materiality, through its own physicality, acts as a structuring aspect of human action. The property of acting, the ability to operate (usually expressed by the term agency), previously reserved for the human, is now extended to material culture suggesting a connection and, why not, a more symmetrical coexistence between the various dimensions of reality. It is in this coexistence that the material and society create each other (Hicks and Beaudry 2010; Olsen 2003; Boivin 2004; 2008).

These are recent proposals in the field of material culture studies, which make the little theorisation about them understandable. In some other fields, however, the same impetus already has a more consolidated trajectory, pointing to the formulation of syntheses. Two of these deserve a quick mention.

Beginning in the 1990s, science and technology studies were gradually fertilised by the sociology of scientific knowledge. One of the consequences was the search for a better understanding of technological objects and their active role in society, as an articulator of action in the same level as human agents. These considerations have occurred, however in the wake of profound philosophical inquiries. A central name here is that of Bruno Latour, a French philosopher and sociologist of science (author, amongst others, of Nous n'avons jamais été modernes, Essai d'anthropologie symétrique, 1991), who proposed that the system of thought with which we have long been accustomed to has promoted an unjustifiable ontological separation between the human and the nonhuman, choosing man as the universal measure and principal agent in the world. However, according to Latour, it was a historically contextualised rupture, established by modern science, albeit with earlier roots. It is a result of a triumph of humanism which exiled nature, the animal world, and the material beyond the frontiers of social action. In pre-modern conceptions, on the contrary, no meaningful distinction could be identified between people and things, between culture and nature. The Actor Network Theory (Theorie de l'Acteur-Réseau), formulated by Latour and others such as Michel Callon and John Law, seeks to reorder the elements that compose reality in a more balanced way, through hybrid compositions, that creates interactions between human and non-human agents. Rather than homogeneous sets (the society of humans, for example), which relates with other more or less static sets (such as the world of objects) the whole of reality is seen as networks where the most heterogeneous actors are associated in changing settings. Entities including social ones exist through relationships. They do not precede them.

In the field of the study of images, similar contributions appeared, above all in the posthumous work of Alfred Gell (Art and agency, an anthropological theory, 1998). Images, according to Gell, cannot be considered merely as reflections of a process involving the creation and transmission of meanings; they are endowed with the attributes of action, they are part of a system that, functioning in a network, generates concrete effects on the agents implied. The vocation of images is to act in society and through their own aesthetic attributes intervene concretely in the course of events. In human behaviour, Gell considers the image (and objects in general) as a secondary agent, whose performance comes from the social action of humans; nevertheless, once it enters the circuit, the elements of its performance belong to it and are not conferred from outside by the perception humans have of them. It is certainly a more moderate position than Latour's, but it points roughly in the same direction, even if Gell was more concerned with the ways in which artistic objects serve as a medium for the performance of human agents.

The impact of the ideas above has considerably altered the agenda of debates in the field of material culture studies, shifting the emphasis from symbolic and representational questions, to the more concrete field of the action of material things and the very materiality of society. Perhaps it is too soon to assess the benefits of such a perspective and equally to weigh the criticisms that are already beginning to emerge. However, it is interesting to invite the historian not to remain insensitive to its implications: in looking at the realities under scrutiny, it is hard to see only human activity in the process of shaping and manipulating a totally inert physical universe. Another perspective and new tools for analysis will be necessary to create historical knowledge that will no longer be only, according to the conventional formula, about man in time, but also about the trajectory of an alive materiality.

'Material culture' is an irremediably ambiguous expression and raises problems by being based on the dichotomy between abstract and physical dimensions of reality and by suggesting that its components arise out from a process of embodiment of an incorporeal phenomenon. Hence, the fallacious contrast with immaterial culture; in both cases, the cultural matrix preceded its expression, which could occur materially or immaterially. A conceptually more adequate definition could help to overcome some of these aphorisms and point out ways for a useful insertion of material culture in the historiographical operation.

Ulpiano Bezerra de Meneses offers some consistent support for a properly historical treatment of material culture. By defining material culture as all that "segment of the physical medium that is socially appropriated by man" (Meneses 1983, 112), he emphasises the human intervention that operates the socialisation of materiality. The notion of appropriation is therefore crucial, since it is through this that society, through culturally established and shared patterns, establishes its multiple interactions with the material universe, shaping it, giving it roles, and meaning. It is not, however, a one-way process, since material culture is understood at the same time as a "product and vector of social relations" (Meneses 1983, 113); a product because it results from human action, from processes of social interactions that create and transform the physical environment; but also vector because it constitutes a concrete support and conductor for effective relations between people. It is useful to stress the fact that there is no univocal cause-and-effect relation that places social relations at the origin of an abstractly conceived process. On the contrary, in the act of its conception, the set of representations, values, and ideas that will subsidise social practices bears the mark of its materiality while in the observer's field of vision. Initiative, the decision to act (agency), appears as an attribute of human actors, and must be recognised as an illusion to which we have become used by the excessive concentration of our attention on human action. Interaction between society and materiality is a two-way street and the set of representations and practices which constitute social action is not conceivable without its physical dimension.

This interaction is still not conceivable without the temporal dimension. It is thus necessary to take in account the dynamics of the transformations which not only human beings—in their dual biological and social condition—go through, but also material culture. In other words, far from forming a static scenario, physical things also have a trajectory, a social life with successive mutations. We could even speak, without any fear of paradox, of a 'biography of things'. In fact, as we have seen, the material world was regarded as something fixed, without its own dynamics, with the only driving force for its transformation being imposed from outside. In this perspective, at the analytical level, things are perceived in a more or less frozen state, as if their existence at any given moment were part of an inherent and perennial condition. Authors such as Arjun Appadurai and Igor Kopytoff have demonstrated, however, that such conditions are transient and that the predominant qualifications in certain moments (for example, that of commodity) express stages of a process (Appadurai 1986). Writing in the 1980s, perhaps these authors may have overemphasised that mutations in the physical universe stem from the attributions of values of a cultural system. What is essential, however, is to retain the extension of temporal dynamics to material things.

The work of the historian intervenes in this succession of states of material culture. Moreover, this occurs in a dual manner: in the first place, because, observing the original context in which things have their social existence, the scholar must be attentive to their mutations, to the fact that material culture. In consonance with all other elements of the society of which it is part, has its historicity. Secondly, the work of analysis itself implies one of these mutations; to consider material culture as a document is to attribute to it a specific value as the bearer of information, placing it, at least provisionally, in a terminal stage. The insertion of the material culture of past societies (and also of the present) into the operation of knowledge presupposes a radical change in the very nature of things, an emptying of the predicates that belonged to them in social contexts, and in the same movement the attribution of other potentialities of an epistemological character. The document only exists, therefore, through the intervention of the historian. Aware of these metamorphoses and their implications, Meneses proposes what is an elementary methodological procedure: 'de-documentalisation,' in other words, through the intermediation of an intellectual act, imagining material culture reinserted in its context, functioning as a socially living thing. In order to, only then, explain its historical role and interactions with people (Meneses 1983, 110). This methodological inversion, which permits moving from the decontextualised document (or better, inserted in other contexts: the museum, the archive, etc.) to the object in its context (or succession of them), applies to, basically, any support of information, whether material or textual, oral or iconographic, although this is not always clear in historiographic work.

A final observation: it is necessary to be cautious to not proceed by simply replacing logocentrism with physicentrism. The insistence on the unique nature of material culture for the proposition of new questions and resolution of others, although positive, must be considered: in the first place, according to its own physical specificity, material culture offers possibilities, but also presents limits, even in comparison with other types of sources. Moreover, any superiority is circumstantial, derived from a strategic advantage created by the kind of inquiry made by the historian. In this sense, potentialities and limits are unequally distributed among the classes of documents, which encourages a diversified and complementary mobilisation in which there is true interaction and not just accumulation. From the heuristic point of view, nothing justifies certain frontiers erected between archaeologists and historians. In the same way that nothing justifies it from the point of view of the realities to be studied. These are only tactical choices, preferences of approach or even capabilities that are distinctly cultivated within each of these disciplines. Similarly, the assertions that material culture offers first-hand access, without the ideological intermediation of writings, thus with greater potential for truth, as well as the evocation of a greater representativeness of material sources, that allows to exceed the narrow limits of literate elites and enter the territory of the less advantaged classes (a 'theoretical democratic advantage' in Prown's words, Prown 1982, 2), are all well-intentioned postulates but must be applied with moderation.

Acknowledgements

The author is grateful to Érika Maynart for translating the original text from Portuguese, and Eoin O'Neill for reviewing the final version.

References

Appadurai, A. ed. 1986. **The social life of things**. Cambridge: Cambridge University Press.

Boivin, N. 2004. Mind over matter? Collapsing the mind-matter dichotomy in material culture studies. In E. DeMarrais et al. eds. **Rethinking materiality. The engagement of mind with material world**. Cambridge: McDonald Institute for Archaeological Research, 63-71.

Boivin, N. 2008. **Material cultures, material minds. The impact of things on human thought, society, and evolution**. Cambridge: Cambridge University Press.

Buchli, V. 2004. Material culture: current problems. In L. Meskell and R. W. Preucel eds. **A companion to social archaeology**. London: Blackwell, 179-194.

Buchli, V. 2004. Introduction, In V. Buchli ed. **The material culture reader**. Oxford: Berg, 1-22.

Csikszentmihalyi, M. 1993. Why we need things. In S. Lubar and W. David Kingery eds. **History from things: assays on material culture**. Washington: Smithsonian institution Press, 20-29.

David, N. and C. Kramer. 2001. Ethnoarchaeology: its nature, origins, and history. In **Ethnoarchaeology in action**. Cambridge: Cambridge University Press, 1-32.

Dittmar, H. 1992. **The social psychology of material possessions**. To have is to be. Hemel Hempstead-New York: Harvester Wheatsheaf-St. Martin's Press.

Douglas, M. B. Isherwood. 1996. **The world of goods. Towards an anthropology of consumption**. London: Routledge.

Harvey, K. 2010. Practical matters. In K. Harvey ed. **History and material culture**. London: Routledge, 1-23.

Hicks D. 2010. The material-cultural turn. Event and effect. In D. Hicks and M. C. Beaudry eds. **The Oxford Handbook of Material Culture Studies**. Oxford: Oxford University Press, 25-98.

Hicks, D. and M. C. Beaudry. 2010. Material culture studies: a reactionary view. In D. Hicks and M. C. Beaudry eds. **The Oxford Handbook of Material Culture Studies**. Oxford: Oxford University Press, 1-21.

Hodder, I. 1982. **Symbols in action**. Cambridge: Cambridge University Press.

Knappett, C. 2005. **Thinking through material culture. An interdisciplinary perspective**. Philadelphia: University of Pennsylvania Press, 2005.

Meneses, U. T. B. de. 1983. A cultura material no estudo das sociedades antigas. **Revista de História**, 115, 103-117.

Miller, D. 1987. **Material culture and mass consumption**. Oxford: Blackwell.

Miller, D. ed. 1998. **Material cultures. Why some things matter**. Chicago: The University of Chicago Press.

Olsen, B. 2003. Material culture after text: remembering things. **Norwegian Archaeological Review**, 36(2), 87-104.

Orser Jr., C. and B. Fagan. 1995. **Historical Archaeology**. New York: HarperCollins.

Pesez, J.-M. 1978. Histoire de la culture matérielle. In J. Le Goff, R. Chartier et J. Revel eds. **La nouvelle histoire**. Paris, Retz, 1978.

Prown, J. D. 1982. Mind in matter: an introduction to material culture theory and method. **Winterthur Portfolio**, 17, 1-19.

Roche, D. 1997. **Histoire des choses banales. Naissance de la consommation, XVIIe – XIXe siècle**. Paris: Fayard.

Schiffer, M. B. 1987. **Formation processes of the archaeological record**. Albuquerque: University of New Mexico Press.

Schnapp, A. 1993. **La conquête du passé. Aux origines de l'archéologie**. Paris: Éditions Carré.

Tilley, C. 1990. **Reading material culture**. Oxford, Blackwell.

Vovelle, M. 1974. **Mourir autrefois**. Paris: Gallimard.

Warnier, J.-P. 1999. **Construire la culture matérielle. L'homme qui pensait avec ses doigts**. Paris: PUF.

Watson, P. J. S Leblanc and C. L. Redman. 1971. **Explanation in archaeology. An explicitly scientific approach**. New York: Columbia University Press.

The acting image and the materialisation of social realities

Carolina Velloza

Introduction

Images in the ancient Near East had a fundamental role in society. They had an ontological attribution that did not distinguish them from reality (Bahrani 2014, 63). In this context, the Amarna Period, which produced such a distinctive iconography, could have promoted significant changes in relevant issues. Images at Amarna were endowed with a constructive power, and might have created relevant social understandings of political and religious views conceived and conveyed by the time of Akhenaten's worldview was introduced.

As modern western scholars, we are placed at a considerable distance in time and mentality from the Amarna Period, which would generate some problems when we attempt to analyse images produced at the time of Akhenaten. It is difficult for us to fully understand their potential to create. This is due to the way we have commonly understood what a reliable source is and what is real itself. That is the main reason why in order to deal with an image we also need to approach it theoretically.

This paper aims to go through the theme based on a theoretical and methodological discussion, which precedes an analysis of images from Armana. The paper is organised in three main sections: (1) 'Some considerations on the trajectory of images as source for the study of the past', where I discuss the origin of the different treatments given to textual and iconographic sources; (2) 'What came into light: methodologies for the analysis of images and material culture', where I try to find clues on how to analyse a pictorial document; and (3) 'Case study: the Amarna Period', where I finally propose an analysis for the images previously discussed.

Some considerations on the trajectory of images as source for the study of the past

As heirs of Greco-Roman rhetoric and the resulting readings of biblical exegesis, historians and other scholars in the humanities are used to accepting that written sources are more rational and more reliable than images and material culture (Hicks and Beaudry 2010; Rede 2012, 133). Our Western way of thinking, Eurocentric in nature (Mignolo 2013), is connected to the belief in a creative, deified word, as we can see in the opening verse of the Gospel of John: "In the beginning was the Word, and the Word was with God, and the Word was God" (John 1:1).

The word is essentially opposed to the image, what implies a contrast between a creative power and a reflective representation of it. That distinction derived from a dual understanding of the world itself (Viveiros de Castro 2012, 162; Viveiros de Castro 2014, 116–117). As a consequence, images and words became part of different fields (Bahrani 2014, 51), and were considered to have different social implications. Images represent things; words produce them. This is a deeply rooted mind-set, both in our minds and in our respective academic backgrounds. Because of this view, texts have been empowered, while historical studies still need to consider the whole potential of images.

Textual sources—as institutionalised by Positivism in the early 19th century—remained for a long time the only sufficiently rational document historical studies could rely upon. Images, on the other hand, were understood as something arising from aesthetic whims, and relegated to catalogues illustrating works in archaeology and art history (Meneses 2003, 13). This created a distinction between what was, and what was not, accepted as art (Freedberg 1989, XIX). In this context images were understood based on two main senses. Firstly, an image could be a phenomenon in itself, something detached from the rest of the world—a pure aesthetic exponent, arising from someone's genius. Secondly, it could be a social mirror—a perfect reflection of what was happening in some part of the world (Meneses 2012, 246).

These deeply rooted beliefs affected not only historiography, but permeated a range of other sciences. The reason can be found in its origins: a way of perceiving social relations and societies according to which objects and images possessed only physical and aesthetic attributes and nothing else. More complex approaches of them, such as studies of temporal and social dynamics and contexts, were marginalised in these cases.

For historians in particular, the lack of more complex approaches certainly had at least two implications. Firstly, historians disregarded or failed to recognise the importance of material culture studies—i.e. texts were considered as sources from which to approach the past, while objects were seen as mere decoration. Secondly, even when recognising the importance of material remains, these historians were not able to effectively incorporate this type of source into their processes of generating—images, even when used, served as an illustration of what the word had already created.

Thus, the established mind-set created a biased hierarchy between words and images. This mentality was derived from how art was conceived in the Western Renaissance (Bahrani 2014, 8; Belting 1994 XXI; Friedberg 1989, II; Mignolo 2013). In the 20th century, scholars started to question such a perspective.

Scholars then started to reassess the role of objects and images (Rede 2012, 136). The most significant revisions appeared in the fields of anthropology, sociology, art history, media and communication studies, linguistics, and semiotics (Schiffer 1999, 4–5; Chilton 1999; Hodder 1989; Latour 1991; Leroi-Gourhan 1993; Lemmonier 1992; 1993; Nöth 1995). In their own particular ways, all these areas of knowledge identified the need to revise our definitions of art (Gell 1998, 12; Mauss 1993, 9). They agreed on the importance of considering the contexts in which to insert images and the implications of the way each image is produced and disseminated (Attfield 2000, 40–41). Finally, they admitted that images also had a trajectory of their own—more than that, they have history.

What came into light: methodologies for the analysis of images and material culture

The following discussions emerged from modern critiques to the way images and material culture were approached in the past produced distinctive methodologies concerned with the inclusion of images in historical analyses, the most outstanding examples being iconography and semiotics (Mahíques 2009). As a critique to the formalism of art history (Meneses 2012, 244), there were new attempts to improve the use of images as a source for the study of the past. Basically these perspectives started to consider images as social phenomena. Iconography has then been raised to the same status as texts.

Influenced by French Structuralism and by linguistic studies (Rede 2101, 138), semiotics proposed that images should be taken as a compound of words in a text—images could then be read as texts. Each icon was a sign, each sign was part of a complex meaning. Thus, semiotics assumed that images conveyed a message that could be unveiled by putting together small units that carried only part of the meaning (Gell 1998, 25). To semiotics, an image was a communicative system, a text displayed in a new platform.

Specialised scholarship started to notice that studying images was not just a matter of including them on the horizon of possible sources from which to do research (e.g. Belting 1994; Friedberg 1989; Gell 1998). Neither was it a matter of taking blind advantage of the same methodology applied to texts. If we wanted to understand societies which produced complex iconographic expressions, such as ancient Egypt, we should consider an image in all its particularities. Images would have, most likely, a different nature than that of texts, while keeping the same creative power it evoked. This perspective started a movement known as "iconic turn" or "pictorial turn", terms first used by W. J. T. Mitchell in the United States and Gottfried Boehm in Germany (Bahrani 2014, 57).

Images are not just a kind of physical or mental support to already existing ideas. It is not in any case neutral or contemplative (Merleau-Ponty 2004, 23). Images are perceived by us in a special way; they interact with us in order to change things: "images are not only on the wall or in the television screen, nor are they only in our heads: they happen, they take place (...)" (Belting 1994, 13). As Freedberg (1989, II) once said, images have a presence, with authority and power. Follwing Gell's definition, images are a social agent or an object imbued with agency—in other words, an image is a constructive power, something that both shapes society and is shaped by it. In the same manner of a social actor that interrelates with other social actors, it is both cause and consequence of important events that could interact with the world, change it, build a new one, or even do it all at the same time (Gell 1998, 8).

Taking this explanation into account, once one starts accepting that an image has its own power, what is the best way to approach it methodologically? How can we truly consider an image a powerful object, both past and present?

A good first step would be recognising that this is a complex task to be undertaken, and a researcher could do is building an image reference survey, something that would create a sort of panorama of elements that may help us start asking questions. In this sense, Meneses proposes the recognition of a specific space where images are created and at the same time create culture—what he calls a visual universe. Meneses also believes that three subcategories compose this universe: the "visual", the "visible" and the "vision" (Meneses 2005, 2 passim).

Once one's object of study is defined, the next step would be to delimitate the iconosphere—i.e., collect referential images produced by the society one is investigating, which could be taken as representative examples of the ways things were depicted. Then we must consider the contexts where images circulated and the possibilities for their reproduction and interaction with members of society. The "visual" is a reminder that images possess a social background (cf. Fyfe & Law 1988), which is responsible not only for defining their insertion in society and ways they would circulate, but also its impact in society. Images themselves hide and deliver facts and factors, detect roles, create or reshape hierarchies, and can even naturalise events—often in a way not understood at first sight. Once we have chosen the range of images to be considered, the next step is defining what is "visible" on them. That is the interaction field between what we see, the context we know about, what the image actually shows, and what we do not see (in the light of what is expected).

Finally, "vision" concerns the audience. The observer eye can also perceive various forms, as well as different ways to interact with an image. Not only does the viewer see an image, but also the image provokes on them some kind of feeling, memory or association. A further task would be determining to what extent we are able to access what past actors saw and how they behave in the light of what images provoked on them. These considerations aim to make us able to face a pictorial source knowing what to look for. However, it is necessary to keep in mind that these procedures are not fixed, as it impossible to propose a rigid methodology for analysing images.

Images of the Amarna Period

Ancient Egyipan images usually conveyed very specific, detailed meanings related to complex mythological narratives or nuanced ways of reaffirming power. The reason for that relies on the Egyptians' continuous emphasis on materiality as a way of reinforcing, creating and sustaining life. In

Meskel's words:

"Statues, figurines, carved and painted images of the individual were all doubles for the self that could extend the biography and trajectory of the individual. The images were the bearers of the owner's identity, personality and visual likeness, and could be called upon as references in the afterlife. These material renderings also had the power to improve upon reality, such as portraying a person as youthful, beautiful and without imperfections. The physical reality of the depiction was thought to have such efficacy as to bestow that desired corporeality upon the person at death as they entered a new domain of existence. If any harm were to befall the deceased's body, those doubles would also physically substitute for his person and guarantee a successful embodied afterlife" (Meskell 2004, 7)

In such a context, one can imagine that images in Amarna Period played an distinctive role in introducing new worldviews, with the change from the emphasis on Amun to the prominent role of the Aten as main god. Akhenaten's reign is usually referred to, in historiography, as a parenthesis in history. However, in order to undertake the difficult task of understanding the role of images in that period, one should take into account the historical background which favoured the occurrence of changes.

Images produced in the very beginning of Akhenaten's reign followed the traditional canon, at least when one considers the more apparent official sources from Thebes. The reign's turning point appears to take place in years four and five, coinciding with the transfer of capital to Amarna—although Akhenaten's project had already started, in a sense, in year one of his reign (Laboury 2010, 101).

The iconography of the Amarna Period is largely recognised for its significant and visible changes in the way characters were depicted, as well as a new repertoire of scenes. According to Aldred (1973, 11), these very unusual images are all dated between in years four and twelve. Among the most significant stylistic changes are the elongated body forms and the absence of linear outlines, among others. The changes introduced by Akhenaten in iconography include:

1) Akhenaten and Nefertiti are represented in an androgynous manner, a fact that has been interpreted in the past as associated to medical disorders (Spiecer and Sprumont 2004, 168). The royal couple is shown with a prominent paunch, wide hips, slim and long fingers, protruding chest, thick lips and effeminate face. Some images depict the king and queen in such a way that is difficult to determine their identity (e.g. Cleveland Museum of Art 59.188; Brooklyn Museum L69.38.1; Brooklyn Museum 60.197.2; Aldred 1973, 109; 111; 193). The figures of Akhenaten and Nefertiti have often been confused for political reasons (Reeves 1999, 88).

2) the presence and prominent role of the royal couple's children, especially their eldest child, Meritaten (e.g. Ägyptisches Museum und Papyrussammlung 14145; Museum of Fine Arts 67.637; Egyptian Museum Cairo JT30/10/26/12; Freed, Markowitz and D'auria 1999, 220; 225; 226).

3) the constant presence of the Aten, depicted above the pharaoh and the royal family in all official scenes. In rare scenes where Akhenaten is depicted without the Aten, other members of the royal family are not shown (e.g. Egyptian Museum Cairo JE 59294; Musée Royaux D'Art et Histoire Brussels E 3051; Aldred 1973, 98–99; 96).

4) the Aten is presented as the Sun Disk, not as an anthropomorphic god. Sometimes the rays emanating from the Sun end up in hands holding *ankh* signs. The Aten's rays always touch the pharaoh, and, sometimes, Nefertiti and other members of the royal family (e.g. Fitzwilliam Museum 2300.1943;

Mourning scene, room gamma, wall B, Amarna Royal Tomb; Presentation of tribute scene, tomb of Meryra II; Aldred 1973, 97; Freed, Markowitz and D'Auria 1999, 31; 89; Martin 1989, pl. 68; Davies 1905, pl. XXXVII). Ordinary people are not depicted in the presence of the Aten (e.g. Museum of Man, San Diego 14881; British Museum EA 343; Aldred 1973, 141; Freed, Markowitz and D'auria 1999, 27), except in very rare examples (Ägyptisches Museum und Papyrussammlung 14123, Freed, Markowitz and D'auria 1999, 271).

6) Although all human figures depicted in Amarna iconography display changes in body and facial features, images where the royal family is absent human characters are usually shown much more conventional ways if compared to the typical Amarna style (e.g. Cleveland Museum of Art 59.187; Scottish Museum 1963.240; Aldred 1973, 122).

Having defined some of the general particularities of images from Amarna derived from a large sample of catalogued images (Aldred 1973; Freed, Markowitz and D'auria 1999), it is now possible to move forward with this pilot study of Amarna images. Two images were selected as an experiment They are considered as references of the relationship between the pharaoh and the Aten. They serve as basis for a trial analysis, which aims to explore agency, power and performance. Emphasis lies upon the aesthetic and visual aspects of representation—reason why the lines do not focus on the inscriptions originally present on those images).

Figure 1: stela Cairo JE 44865. Drawing by F. A. Vieira (after Freed, Markowitz and D'Auria 1999, 106)

Figure 1 is a scene carved in a limestone stela, 43.5 cm high. The scene dates prior to year 9 of Akhenaten's reign. Inscriptions showing the names of the king, the queen, their daughters, and the Aten can be seen in the top and side frames, as well as over the royal couple's heads. This bas-relief shows the royal couple and three of their daughters (Merytaten, Mekataten and Ankhesenpaten). The king and queen are sitting facing each other in cushioned seats, wearing sandals, with both their feet supported by a hassock. The princesses apparently play with their parents. Akhenaten gives a jewel to his eldest daughter, which possibly emulates the shape of the Sun Disk, whose rays only touch the royal couple (Arnold 1996, 101; Chapot 2015, 507). A kiosk surrounds the family. Detailed features are described in the analytical table below:

Character	Section	Description
Akhenaten	Body and face form	Prominent paunch. His body features are elongated and effeminate. His chin is pointed and long; his nose is round and large. His ears draw attention by its size. His lips are pouty. His body has curves and exaggerated lines, just as his wider hips. On his chest, a prominence suggests small breasts. His neck is very long. His body position is very delicate
	Clothing	Naked torso, partially covered only by a collar on his shoulders. He wears a long skirt
	Crown	Blue crown with *uraeus* and ribbons
	Position	The king sits on the left-hand side. His right arm is stretched to the side of his body, while his left arm is bent. In his left hand there is a jewel, which he gives to Merytaten
Nefertiti	Body and face form	The queen is depicted in a more delicate way as the king, although bears the same characteristics of Akhenaten's representation
	Clothing	The clothes she wears are very similar to his, with the difference that hers cover her chest, are tighter and have a pending tissue
	Crown	The queen wears her typical flat-topped crown with *uraeus*
	Position	The queen sits on the right-hand side. Although her throne is different, Nefertiti is depicted with the same proportions as Akhenaten. Just like him, she sits gently and looks directly to the front, towards her husband. Unlike Akhenaten, she holds two of her daughters on her lap
Daughters	General considerations	Merytaten is standing between Akhenaten and Nefertiti. The other two are sit on their mother's lap. Akhenaten holds a jewel to Merytaten, while Nefertiti touches her head. Mekataten and Ankhesenpaten also appear to play. All of them are naked
Aten	General Considerations	In the top register of the scene, as a solar disc with rays ending up in hands which give life

Figure 2: relief fragment Berlin ÄM 14511. Drawing by F. A. Vieira (after Arnold 1996, 104).

Figure 2 is also a scene from house stela in painted limestone, 12 cm high, from Amarna, dating from somewhere between the year twelve and fifteen. The fragmentary scene reveals the royal couple's heads, under the Aten's rays. According to Aldred (1973, 69), the whole scene must have shown Akhenaten sitting on a throne, with a supporting elbow, while Nefertiti was standing before him, leaning forward to put a necklace or breastplate around his neck. As before, detailed outstanding features are described in the analytical table below:

Character	Section	Description
Akhenaten	Body and face forms	Effeminate and androgynous traits (pointed chin, broad nose, big ears and a face with accentuated curves)
	Clothing	Not enough information
	Crown	Blue crown with *uraeus* and ribbons
	Position	His right arm folded behind his head
Nefertiti	Body and face forms	Delicate face features, pointed chin and accentuated curves
	Clothing	Not enough information

	Crown	She appears with her typical flat-topped crown
	Position	The queen involves the king with her arms in a loving embrace, probably to present him with a ceremonial necklace. The king and queen are so close that their noses are touching, almost kissing
Aten	General Considerations	In the top register of the scene, as a solar disc with rays ending up in hands

The preliminary description consists of a first step towards a complete examination of an image. It offers us clues about different issues, depending on both the source we use and the questions we ask. As mentioned before, the primary interest here is to understand the relationship between the pharaoh and the god Aten. The basic questions to ask are: how is the pharaoh depicted in these images? And how is the god depicted?

In both figures 1 and 2, pharaoh Akhenaten is represented as an androgynous and effeminate figure. His body presents very noticeable curves, and exaggerated shapes characterise his face. The skirt he wears marks his hips and prominent paunch (figure 1). The Aten is depicted on top of the heads of the royal family, with rays ending up in hands which give life. The Sun Disk is placed on top of the centre of the complete scene, providing a notion of symmetry. The position of the figures of the Aten, Akhenaten and Nefertiti also create the impression of circular construction of spaces of representation (figure 1) (Davis 1989, 32).

Egyptian canonical iconography traditionally represented hierarchies in its images, showing different characters in different positions and sizes (Ziegler and Bovot 2001, 28). The representation of the king was always larger than other human figures. The gods were also represented in a more prominet way than the king. Likewise, kings and gods occupied a privileged place in the scene, either more central or higher. A first consideration of figures 1 and 2 would reveal that this rule is respected, with Akhenaten depicted under the Aten. In a more detailed analysis, however, things do not seem to be that straightforward.

Considering the fact that figure 1 presents two main human characters as symmetrical figures. It is possible to say that symmetry tends to emphasise and equalise things, expressing resemblance. In figure 1, Akhenaten is the symmetric pair of Nefertiti. This means that, in a way, they are peers. This fact is something to be considered. Iconographically, the king is equivalent to the queen, something at least unusual in the Egyptian canonical art (Ziegler and Bovot 2001, 40). Apart from differences such as body form and garments, both the images of Akhenaten and Nefertiti have a lot in common. Their posture and attire, the places they occupy and the size of their representations—especially in comparison to other characters in the scene. The symmetry and rapprochement between the characters is highly visible. However, what is invisible in this image is the fact that this is not a common scenario in Egyptian images as mentioned before (i.e. it represents a break with tradition).

The Aten is placed in the exact centre of the image. The god's representation experiences no clear symmetrical relationship with other characters. In other words, he is equivalent to himself. One might say that this is a final proof of the god's superior qualities, since he is equal only to himself while the king, on the other hand, is equal to the queen. This leads us to the conclusion that the relationship between the god and the pharaoh is unchanged, although the relationship between the king and queen should be studied further for better understanding.

Other image elements, however, might suggest a more complex explanation. For example, the construction of a highly geometrical representation of the god. In both figures 1 and 2, the Aten is seen as an abstract circular shape. Once we have seen this figure and recognised its centrality, one would assume its highly important role in the scene.

However, the very abstract circular form of god is constructed in a way that directs our gaze below, towards the royal couple. The Sun rays point us the king, or rather, to be more accurate, the symmetrical representation of the royal couple. In other words, the allegedly most important figure of the stela leads us to the king.

Once more, what emerges from this analysis is a relevant situation, both from what we see and what we do not see. The god, the central figure, presents us the king, not the other way around, and that is precisely what we cannot see. What figure 1 suggests, when considering other canonical Egyptian representations, is that we have a clear inversion in the direction of our gaze, from the god to the king, not from the king to the god. The traditional direction of observation reinforces a hierarchy between god and king—the later serves and worships the former, not the other way around. On the contrary, the composition of Amarna scenes suggests a modification on the way the hierarchy between god and king was perceived.

How different would this new hierarchical relation between god and king be? It is the god that leads us to see the king and not the opposite. On one hand, the god occupies a privileged position in the image, but, on the other hand, from the perspective of the god, the more privileged one is precisely the pharaoh. This also suggested in the Great Hymn to the Aten:

"You are in my heart,

and there is no other who knows you

except for your son (Nefer-kheperu-Re Wa-en-Re),

for you have apprised him of your designs and your

power (…)" (Simpson 2003, 283).

It is only Akhenaten, the king, who knows the god, his father, who—according to the same document—is the provider of life (Simpson 2003, 278):

"(…) You rise in perfection on the horizon of the sky,

living Aten, who determines life.

Whenever you are risen upon the eastern horizon

you fill every land with your perfection. (…)" (Simpson 2003, 283).

Thus, Akhenaten's exclusive knowledge of a powerful god, indicates that he is the only one who knows the Aten, who, therefore, emphasises Akhenaten as a privileged individual in the same way it is depicted in figures 1 and 2 (as the sunrays only touch him and Nefertiti). Would that be a suggestion of some sort of equivalence between god and king? Considering this is true, it could show the god's desire to present and boast the king, who is very important to him.

One might say that the god presents not only the king, but also the queen. Figure 1 shows that the Aten's rays touch only the king and the queen, even when there are other characters in the scene, such as the princesses. In figure 2, the queen performs an honourable task, a kind of consecration that could be described as divine (Bryan 1998, 51–52), as she honours the king for his merits during his life.

Additionally, the androgyny of both Akhenaten and Nefertiti could suggest an equivalence (between them. In this way, a circular movement that encompasses three divine beings represented in these scenes is potentially revealed: from the queen to the king; from the king to the god; from back to the royal couple. If that is true, these images could indicate a new balance between the figures of the pharaoh and the great royal wife, as well as another meaning given to the king's authority before the god Aten. Akhenaten is, as suggested, a king adored by his own god, a king with ruling powers before the Aten who is, in turn, the only mentioned god existing. This is no banal change, which would indicate an exponential increase of the pharaoh's power.

Conclusion

In order to securely determine that the Amarna Period presented a change in the authority of the pharaoh and the role of the main divinity, a wider range of sources would have to be analysed. The analysis presented here does not expect to provide final answers; rather, it aimed to explore and test other ideas surrounding Akhenaten's revolution and the role played by the pharaoh and his new god. Hopefully, this paper has shown the huge potential of images to uncover other aspects of the Amarna Period, especially regarding Akhenaten's increase of power. Long known sources from the Amarna Period still hold the potential to produce new insights.

References

Aldred, C. 1973. **Akhenaten and Nefertiti**. New York: Viking Press.

Arnold, D. 1996. **The Royal Woman of Amarna. Images of Beauty from Ancient Egypt**. New York: Metropolitan Museum of Art.

Attfield, J. 2000. **Wild Things: Material Culture of everyday Life**. Oxford: Berg.

Belting, H. 1994. **Likeness and Presence: a history of the image before the Era of Art**. London: The University of Chicago Press.

Bryan, B. 1998. Antecedents to Amenhotep III. In D. O'Connor and E. H. Cline eds. **Amenhotep III: Perspectives on his Reign**. Ann Arbor: The University of Michigan Press, 27–62.

Chapot, G. 2015. **A Família Real Amarniana e a Construção de uma Nova Visão de Mundo Durante o Reinado de Akhenaton**. Unpublished PhD Thesis. Niterói: Universidade Federal Fluminense.

Chilton, E. ed. 1999. **Material Meanings: Critical Approaches to the Interpretation of Material Culture**. Salt Lake City: University of Utah Press.

Davies, N. de G. 1905. **The Rock Tombs of El Amarna 2**. London: Egypt Exploration Society.

Davis, W. 1989. **The Canonical Tradition in Ancient Egyptian Art**. Cambridge: Cambridge

University Press.

Freed, R., Y. Markowitz and S. D'Auria eds. 1999. **Pharaohs of the Sun, Akhenaten, Nefertiti and Tutankhamun**. London: Thames &Hudson.

Freedberg, D. 1989. **The Power of Images: Studies in the History and Theory of Response**. Chicago: The University of Chicago Press.

Fyfe, G., J. Law eds. 1988. **Picturing Power: Visual Depiction and Social Relations**. London: Routledge.

Gell, A. 1998. **Art and Agency: an Anthropological Theory**. Oxford: Oxford University Press.

Hicks, D. and M. C. Beaudry. 2010. Material Culture Studies: a Reactionary View. In D. Hicks and M. C. Beaudry eds. **The Oxford Handbook of Material Culture Studies**. Oxford: Oxford University Press, 1–21.

Hodder, I. ed. 1989. **The Meanings of Things: Material Culture and Symbolic Expression**. London: HarperCollins.

Laboury, D. 2010. **Akhénaton**. Paris: Pygmalion.

Latour, B. 1991. **We Have Never Been Modern**. Cambridge, Mass: Harvard University Press.

Lemmonnier, P. 1992. **Elements for an Anthropology of Technology**. Ann Arbor: University of Michigan Press.

Leroi-Gourhan, A. 1993. **Gesture and Speech**. Cambridge, Mass: MIT Press.

Mahiques, R. G. 2008. **Iconografía e Iconología. Volumen 1: La Historia del Arte como Historia Cultural**. Madrid: Ediciones Encontros.

Freed, Y. Markowitz and S. D'Auria eds. 1999. **Pharaohs of the Sun, Akhenaten, Nefertiti and Tutankhamun**. London: Thames &Hudson

Martin, G. T. 1989. **The Royal Tomb of El-'Amarna**. Vol. 2. London: Egypt Exploration Society.

Mauss, M. 1993. **Manual de Etnografia**. Lisboa: Don Quixote.

Meneses, U. T. B. de. 2003. Fontes Visuais, Cultura Visual, História Visual. Balanço Provisório, Propostas Cautelares. **Revista Brasileira de História**, 23(45), 11–36.

Meneses, U. T. B. de. 2005. Rumo à uma História Visual. In: J. de. S. Martins ed. **O Imaginário e o Poético nas Ciências Sociais**. Bauru: EDUSC.

Meneses, U. T. B. de. 2012. História e Imagem: Iconografia/Iconologia e Além. In: C. F. Cardoso e R. Vainfas eds. **Novos Domínios da História**. São Paulo: Elsevier, pp. 243- 262.

Merleau-Ponty, M. 1948. **Conversas**. São Paulo: Martins Fontes.

Meskell, L. 2004. **Object Wolds in Ancient Egypt: Material Biographics Past and Present**. Oxford: Berg.

Mignolo, W. 2013. Decolonialidade como o Caminho para a Cooperação. **Revista do Instituto Humanitas Unisinos**, 431 (online).

Nöth, W. 1995. **Handbook of Semiotics**. Indianapolis: Indiana University Press.

Rede, M. 2012. História e Cultura Material. In: C. F. Cardoso e R. Vainfas eds. **Novos Domínios da História**. São Paulo: Elsevier, pp. 133–150.

Reeves, N. 1999. The Royal Family. In R. Freed, Y. Markowitz and S. D'Auria eds. **Pharaohs of the Sun, Akhenaten, Nefertiti and Tutankhamun**. London: Thames &Hudson, 81–96.

Schiffer. M. B. 1999. **The Material Life of Human Beings**. London: Routledge.

Simpson, W. K. ed. 2003 **The Literature of Ancient Egtpt, An Anthology of Stories, Instructions, Stelae, Autobiographies, and Poetry**. New Haven: Yale University Press.

Spiecer, C. and P. Sprumont. 2004. La construction de l'image du corps de l'élite égyptienne à l'époque amarnienne. **Bulletins et mémoires de la Societé d'Anthropologie de Paris**, 16(3–4), 167–185.

Viveiros de Castro, E. 2012. Transformação na Antropologia, transformação da Antropologia. **Mana**, 18(1), 151–171.

Viveiros de Castro, E. 2014. **Cannibal Metaphysics: for a Post-Structural Anthropology**. Minneapolis, Minnesota: Univocal.

Ziegler, C. and J.-L. Bovot. 2001. **Art et archéologie: l'Égypte ancienne**. Paris: École du Louvre.

Agency and representation of Nubians in Egyptian iconography in the 18th Dynasty: ethnic strategies and negotiations

Fábio Amorim Vieira

Introduction: Nubia in Egyptology and the urgency of ethnicity

In 1829, Jean-François Champollion sent a letter to his brother Jacques-Joseph depicting everything he saw while travelling for fifteen days in the Nubian lands of Egypt. During a visit to the Ramesside temples of Abu Simbel, Champollion used the following words to describe a painted scene of Nubian captives chained to one another under Ramses II: 'two lines of African prisoners, some of Negro race and others of Barabra race, forming groups perfectly designed, full of effect and life' (Champollion 1833, 133). This quote from Champollion's letter reflects an emblematic perspective of Nubia in modern Egyptology.

Egyptology has been closely connected with colonialist and imperialist agendas during the 19th and 20th centuries. According to the Western perspective, human differences in past periods can easily be compared and explained by how modern anthropological dissimilarities were seen by people living in these periods. Consequently, studies concerning the ancient Egyptian society and its neighbouring communities have often constructed misleading correlations between ethnic differentiations of the ancient world and modern racial concepts. Accordingly, Egyptologists have defined Nubians as coming from south of the borders of Egypt in racial categories in a similar way (Smith 2007, 220), as the letter of Champollion clearly shows above. Egyptian material culture often describes foreigners in Egypt as potential enemies or subdued prisoners, an idea that is directly linked to the racial perspective of Nubian inferiority. These interpretations follow an academic perspective that recognises the contact areas between Egypt and Nubia in terms of a one-way confluence, emphasising Nubian history of subjugation under Egyptian rule.

On the other hand, recent studies have sought to understand the relations between Nubia and Egypt in a way that highlights the entanglements between diverse cultural elements, power hierarchies, and subservience. Concomitant with these new perspectives, postcolonial theories have emerged criticising knowledge-producing models that still replicate a colonial view of the past. Nevertheless, it is indispensable to mention that the *colonial* suffix in *postcolonial* is not only related to the recent political experience, but also to several other historical events of oppression and delimitation of boundaries (Costa 2006, 117–118). The postcolonial approach may thus be considered as an analytical operation for the recognition of colonial hierarchies. As a consequence of applying this outlook to the Nubian situation in the period under Egyptian colonial rule, resilience and survival strategies are emphasised and raise new cultural perspectives yearning for the agency of Nubians in the context of Egyptian domination over Nubia.

Following the writings of Fredrik Barth and other anthropologists who wrote in the last decades of the 20th century, ethnicity is now seen as a social construct of subjective and permeable identities and boundaries. However, in contrast to other areas of Archaeology or Classics, Egyptology still is in its infancy with respect to exploring the anthropological concept of ethnicity (Riggs and Baines 2012, 1).

According to Barth (2011, 195–197), the delimitation of boundaries between 'us' and 'them' marks inclusions and exclusions that will define borders that may vary by internal and external social dealings of multiple cultural elements. Similarly, ethnic groups represent categories of resemblance and identification, whose attribution is made by their own actors (Barth 2011, 189). As a construct that depends on its subjects, ethnicity also depends on the interactions of the subjects.

From a perspective of ethnic correlations and cultural changes, this article aims to approach Nubian agency in Egyptian iconography from the dawn of the New Kingdom. According to Geertz (1989), and considering 'culture' as a web of significance woven by humans, we herein seek to interpret these patterns of meanings as composing cultural Egyptian iconographic elements of Nubia. Egyptian images express views and perspectives characteristic of Egyptian cultural contexts. Therefore, iconography consists of a relevant source to acknowledge that the components of the material life of ancient Egyptians and Nubians are 'inflected with social relations and thus can be read as a window onto larger cultural structures' (Meskell 2004, 15).

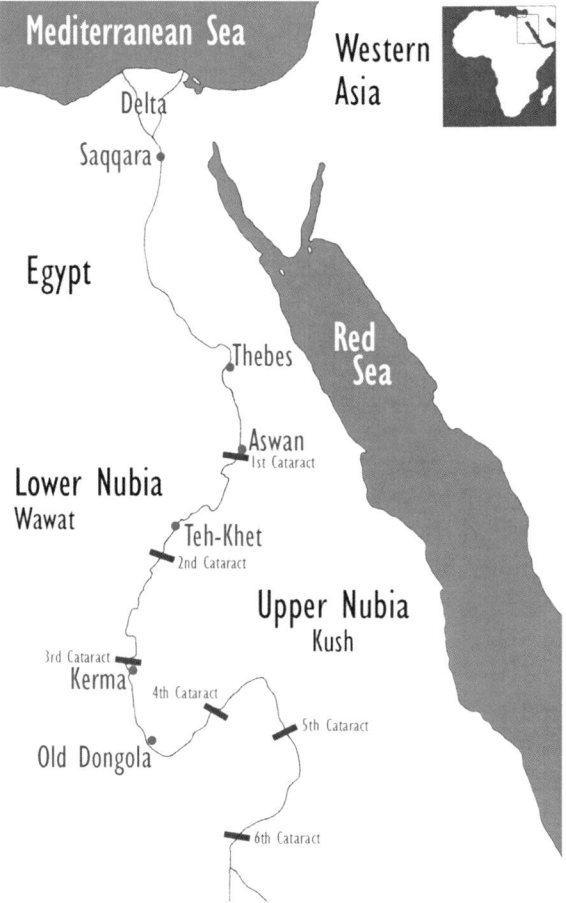

Figure 1: Map of Egypt and the lower and upper areas of Nubia. Map by the author.

Egypt and Nubia at the dawn of the New Kingdom

During the New Kingdom (1550–1050 BC), the number of foreigners in Egypt increased significantly. After being dominated for more than a century by the Hyksos, Egyptian worldviews changed as a result of a closer relationship between Egypt and its neighbours, both from southern border and Asia (O'Connor 1983, 194). The cosmopolitan and diversified nature of Egyptian society during the New Kingdom is also attested in bioarchaeological evidence from capital cities such as Amarna, which includes variation in cranial morphology and marks of stress of uncertainty (Dabbs and Zakrzewski 2011, 199; Dabbs et al 2015, 40).

From a political perspective, it is important to understand Nubia as an assembly of multiple political organisations and heterogeneous populations. While Egypt was a kingdom that had been unified long before, the vast lands of Nubia, situated between the first and the sixth cataracts of the river Nile, were composed by correlated groups and independent chiefdoms (Kemp 2006, 319).

It is also important to point out that Nubian regions had strong economical and political relations with Pharaonic lands controlled by the Hyksos, and that the commercial exchange between the north and Egyptians in the south was confirmed by the material culture of Thebes present in Nubian areas such as Kerma (Török 2009, 107).

In general, both military and administrative groups had full knowledge of the region placed between the first and the second cataract of the river Nile named Wawat (Lower Nubia). As a consequence of the re-conquest of the areas between the second and the fifth cataract, the Egyptians were also able to settle in Kush (Upper Nubia).

The Theban Pharaohs focused primarily on the southern regions of Nubia in an attempt to dismantle the political supremacy of Kerma and to re-establish Pharaonic control in Lower Nubia during the Egyptian uprising against their enemies. Inscriptions in Arminna and Toshka in Lower Nubia report the Egyptian recovery of these sites and the subsequent control by Egyptian officials by the end of the 17th Dynasty (Török 2009, 111).

Pharaohs of the 18th Dynasty sent armies to Nubia in order to regain territorial control and exploit natural recourses (Morkot 2000), which resulted in the viceroyalty of Nubia. Faced with an administrative system of Egyptian authority, Nubian territories received scribes, priests, officials, and artisans that worked for a government ruled by an indirect administration, in which an Egyptian viceroy was designated by the Pharaoh to rule and control the local chiefs (Kemp 1979).

During this period, campaigns for the territorial conquest resumed and intensified, and, as the Egyptian military forces conquered the southern regions of Nubia (Arrais 2011), the clash between cultures resulted in more negative and idealized stereotypes and representations of the Nubians in Egyptian iconography (see Anthony 2017). In addition, discourses of Egyptian superiority (and non-inferiority) appeared in official texts, as well as images to ensure symbolic Egyptian rule over the foreigners (Kemp 1979, 8; Smith 2007).

Egyptian official otherness: topical images of Nubians

Egyptian texts and images provide an overbearing view of how control and subordination of other regions and people were maintained under Pharaonic colonial domination. These portrayals are directly linked to how the expansionist power worked, and represent powerful elements of social struggle that weave mental images or social manifestations that are destined to maintain these images (Bourdieu 1996, 108). Their consequences are compelling and impose certain worldviews that create and dissolve groups.

The dawn of the expansion of the Egyptian frontier during the 18th Dynasty generated numerous official portraits of kings slaughtering enemies—a common scene in Predynastic iconography since the Narmer Palette. However, the ethnic and expansionist character of this period reflects directly on the records and how the enemies were identified and stereotyped. From this perspective, the enemies are clearly distinguishable in battle scenes, in which the Pharaoh advances with bow and arrow, attacking a chaotic crowd (referred to in inscriptions as the 'wretched Kush'), while the members of the crowd exhibit hair, clothes, and skin colour that match the Egyptian representation criteria of Nubians (figure 2).

Figure 2: A sketch of a scene from a painted wood box from the tomb of Tutankhamun, depicting the pharaoh fighting against Nubian enemies. Drawing by the author.

Reflected in battles and political plans of domination, stereotypical definitions remind us how the borders raised by the Egyptians between themselves and the Nubians show cultural contrasts in Egypto-Nubian interactions in terms of position, superiority, inferiority, and otherness. One of the elements defining otherness is a highly stereotyping ethnic group that insists on a dissonance in a narrow interethnic contact (Barth 2011, 200–201). This element reflects not only a military opposition, but also a cosmogonical view of protection against the enemy. Embodied by the rigid figure of the pharaoh, Egypt fights chaos ('*isfet*'), which is represented by several trampled Nubians. In this context, the pharaoh is considered as keeper of the Egyptian order and justice, *maat*, and the one who should battle against the enemies of the order, which acknowledges the foreign invaders as non-Egyptian agents of chaos (Smith 2007, 223).

Taking into consideration the ideas of Fredrik Barth, for whom ethnic identity is related to a specific cultural set of evaluative archetypes (Barth 2011, 209), it is reasonable to assume that the established differences between Egyptians and other groups can be considered as provided by different evaluation criteria. In this context, coexistence with foreigners and the difference in designations are readily perceived in Pharaonic representations and discourses.

The Egyptians had to elaborate symbols that would legitimate their representation of Nubians both as a threat and as an inferior group. Thus, culture is a maintainer and restorer of ethnic limits based on contrast and differentiation (Barth 2011, 195–197).

Economic features also played a central role in the constitution of Egypto-Nubian interactions. The Egyptian expansion over Nubia targeted valued products such as gold, animal skins, incense, feathers, ostrich eggs, and ivory from south of the border. These elements, apart from their role in trading activities, became important cultural markers in the differentiation of different groups.

Human servants and captives were among the tributes Nubians brought to Egypt. Antonio Loprieno discusses coercive work practices and the captivity of outsiders and war prisoners in territories invaded during the Egyptian expansion, which is documented in military biographical accounts (Loprieno 2012, 8). Tax records in Egypt contain important quantitative information regarding the exploitation of Nubia, as taxes were paid in ivory, gold, ebony, animal skins, crops, servants, and prisoners from Wawat and

Kush (Bianchi 2004, 112-113). When focusing on the taxation of politically subordinated regions, and analysing the iconographic documentation of Egypt, one can see many facets of Nubian transits to Egypt.

Considering ethnic contact as entanglements, one can interpret Egypt, Nubia and their frontiers as matrices of social and political formation. However, it is fundamental to understand the distinction of borders as manifestations of the dynamism given in the subjectivities of ethnic groups. These groups that live in or crossed demarcated lands set the surrounding ethnic frontiers and change the cultural traits through diverse interactive and contrasting experiences which result in the impact of cultural inner and outer elements (Barth 2011, 195–197).

An example of an anonymous portrayal of people being obliged to migrate to Egypt can be found in the Theban tomb of Huy (TT 40). Representations in the tomb show commodities and captives being sent as payment by the Nubians to Egypt, including a ported ship containing five Nubians exhibiting painted hair adorned with typical Nubian feathers, wearing thick hoop earrings, and displaying strips that attach their arms to their neck (Davies and Gardiner 1926, plate XXXI). Such images suggest the transit of these subjects via the Nile, travelling between their original places towards Egypt.

Another picture from the same tomb shows more Nubian prisoners being transferred to Egypt. In this image, two red-haired and dark-skinned women appear with colourful skirts and adorned arms, both carrying children. Right before these figures, a row of five Nubian men with tied hands is shown, coloured and adorned with equipment that has a strong connection to Nubian culture such as ostrich feathers, and clothes made of animal skins (figure 3). It is important to highlight that this exchange of material tributes, captives, and noblemen from Nubia happened as a result of the politics weaved between Horemheb and the Nubian leaderships during Tutankhamun's reign. After notable Nubian revolts, diplomatic negotiations occurred, during which members of the Nubian government from Wawat and Kush went to Egypt to offer tributes and political cordialities to the Egyptian empire (Grimal 2005, 242).

Figure 3: A sketch of a painting on the wall of the Theban tomb of Huy (TT 40), showing Nubian women and prisoners sent to Egypt. Drawing by the author.

In the tomb of Horemheb at Saqqara, there are portraits of captured Nubians ready to be sent to Egyptian areas, which reflects the increasing number of foreigners in Egypt during the 18th Dynasty. Egyptian officials were represented counting the number of prisoners to be sent to Egypt during a mission in the South (figure 4). In another scene, Egyptian scribes register spoils brought from Nubia, and one of the Nubian captives is taken by force to join a crowd seated on the floor near other tributes.

Figure 4: A sketch of a scene on the eastern wall of Horemheb's tomb in Saqqara depicting the counting of Nubian prisoners (EG 1889 Museo Civico Archeologico, Bologna). Drawing by the author.

The tomb images from Thebes and Saqqara indicate the need to conceive the role of foreigners in society became important in Egypt. If the composition of these images contains stereotypical elements that exaggeratingly express the condition of the foreigners, it is evocative to assess the context of inferiority and subjection, in which Nubia is shown in Egyptian iconography. Beyond real aspects, these images as taxonomic patterns have to be interpreted closer to the world of its creators and further away from the world of its subject (Meskell 2004, 40; Anthony 2017, 99). As a result of the perspective shown by these scenes, it is clear that the Egyptian elites and the foreigners officials were only able to display ethnic elements when the stereotypes of strangeness favoured the superiority of Egypt (Smith 2015).

As a conservative society that worried about homogeneous ideals, Egypt pretended to be the maintainer of the order and representation against the chaos and otherness (Riggs and Baines 2012, 2). However, as previously mentioned, the Egyptian elites were familiar with Nubians and defined them through iconography. Considering the experience of Nubian displacement in Egypt, our eyes seek for other ethnic portraits that go beyond the typical representation of Nubian subservience defined by Egyptians.

Elements of negotiation: Nubian everyday life possibilities in Egypt

One of the images in the Theban tomb of the scribe of recruits Haremhab (TT 78) differs from the other paintings that show the stereotypical tied bodies and austerely subordinate Nubians. With adorned arms, ears and neck on a moving body, a Nubian dancer is depicted (Davies and Gardiner 1936, vol. 1, plate XL; figure 5). This representation carries various Nubian elements such as adornments, hair and skin colour that clearly shows his ethnic origin, and opens the possibility that this individual had migrated to Egypt under conditions and circumstances that are not necessarily linked to captivity and forced labour, but may be a result of the voluntary relations between the Nubian elites and the Pharaonic state.

Figure 5: A sketch of Nubian dancer depicted in the tomb of Haremhab (TT 78). Drawing by the author.

Depictions in the tomb of of Tjanuny (TT 74) show individuals whose traits are closely connected to Nubians (Davies MSS 10.27.3; Peck 1971). From the ostrich feathers attached to the hair, largely used in the southern stereotypical representation, to the soldiers' hairstyle, the ethnic references to Nubia are expressive, and suggest the Nubian presence in the Egyptian army. This expresses the tradition of including Nubian men in the army that takes place since the Old and Middle Kingdoms (Lacovara 2001, 20; Arrais 2011, 51). In the same scene, the Nubian soldiers are followed by a percussionist, who plays a set of percussions hanging from his neck (Davies MSS. 10.27.2; Peck 1971;figure 6). Such barrel-shaped drums were played especially by Nubians during military parades or religious processions (Emerit 2013, 5).

Figure 6: A sketch of soldiers and a percussionist in the tomb of Tjanuny (TT 74). Drawing by the author.

Other representations of the same instrument can be found in Egypt and in Nubia. For example, in Lower Nubia, a wall painting in the tomb of Djehutyhotep at Debeira depicts an individual in a musical scene which is remarkably similar to the percussionist in the tomb of Tjanuny (Säve-Söderbergh and Troy 1991, plate I; figure 7). This similarity requires a deeper analysis. Both representations depict considerable similarities and almost identical ethnic elements such as skin colour, hairstyle, clothes, and even the braided pattern instrument. These similarities suggest that both representations depict Nubian percussionists, who worked in Nubia and in Egypt.

Figure 7: A sketch of the musical scene painted in the tomb of Djehutyhotep. Drawing by the author.

Even though captives and servants are present in Egyptian iconography, they remain usually anonymous. This fact allows us to assume the existence of social interchanges between Nubia and Egypt. Even though these captives are represented, they remain anonymous. However, their representation still works as evidence of their movement across North-eastern Africa. There are few documents describing the routine of foreigners in Egypt, and information about these individuals had usually been lost by the time they arrived in Egypt.

Based on information from relatively scarce cases between the Second Intermediate Period and the New Kingdom, Loprieno highlights the possibility of social ascension for these subjects through strategies such as adoption by Egyptian families, marriage with Egyptian citizens, or temple service (Loprieno 2012, 8). From this perspective, it seems likely that these men and women living in Egypt, would have decided to accept and adapt to their new environment as a way to survive. However, if the representations of the Nubian captives that came to Egypt in a context of conquest are followed by an assumed silence or dissolution of their images in Egyptian daily life, stereotypical elements of these populations in other representations (e.g. as soldiers, dancers, and musicians) in Thebes suggest their agency in the negotiations of foreign individuals. A project of domination such as the Egyptian over Nubia incorporates men and women from different origins into a complex mesh of interactions and exchange under official power. This composition includes both elite members and commoners, and through practices of servitude and displacement, foreign people were able to integrate the dominant world. However, this reality of integration has to be seen as influential for both sides of the Egyptian dichotomy.

Acknowledging the agency of these characters contradicts the idea of complete subservience and the impossibility of the existence of foreigners in Egypt, thus antagonizing the projections of the official Pharaonic discourse. Even if scholars have adopted the ideology of these discourses that postulate a growing monolithic and dichotomous analysis of Egyptian over other cultures (Riggs and Baines 2012, 2), it is necessary to perceive their agency as pervaded by acts of negotiation, appropriation, transformation, and resistance (Given 2005, 15). Social sets of power can be interpreted as arenas in which subjects react in a multitude of ways and in different proportions to the imposed power. As far as cultural differences are concerned, complex negotiations emerged, mixed with a complex scenario of tensions and strategies that were imposed by the official order.

In such a context, cultural webs are composed of shared systems of attitudes, values, and meanings as a result of the exchange between the dominant and the subordinate, which is consistent with 'an arena of conflictive elements' (Thompson 1998, 17). Considering the authoritative features of the domination of the outsider in the Egypto-Nubian context, this may constitute evidence for sanctions, appropriations, and possible resistance in Egyptian everyday life in the pictorial representations of Nubians.

Beyond the rigidity of the pre-established cultural traditions, articulations of historical characters marked with distinguishing features emerge from complex negotiations giving legitimacy and historical transformation to new cultural affiliations (Bhabha 2013, 21).

Thus, even if anonymous, such individuals must be faced as emanations of people, whose representations manifest as a reflection of the transformation of the official Egyptian discourse and the opposition to the presence of the foreigners. Such transformation is attested by the subtle rise of authorised versions of otherness (Bhabha 2013, 150–151) and crosses the cultural condition of subaltern existence in the blend of tenacious Nubian elements with the appropriation of Egyptian functions in Pharaonic society, expressed previously through the army, music, and dance. Hence, these partial synchronisations reveal the Egyptian power ambivalence and the acting of the Nubian presence towards the Egyptian iconographic representations. Far from being mere distant images that are disconnected from the actions of reality, these representations are agents in reality themselves and engage meanings and peoples' subjectivities in the potentiality of social structures and of what is established as official within the state (Bourdieu 1996, 112).

Conclusion

Prior to the existence of Egyptian representations denoting processes of identification and distinction, it was possible to interpret the Egyptian perspective towards their southern neighbours as a result of experience, intentions, and movements that built constant cultural interactions. During these distinction processes, contrasting elements of physical and, mainly, cultural meanings displayed more than the expression of otherness linked to subservience. These elements, which are present in the daily life of characters emulating experiences of soldiers, percussionists, or dancers and should thus be interpreted according to the topic vision imposed by Egyptian iconography itself, were analysed as constitutive of the Nubian agency in the Egyptian context. This is, however, an agency that antagonises the Pharaonic discourse of dichotomy between Egyptians and foreigners, and shows synchronisations, negotiations, and a break in the hegemonic structure of the Egyptian culture.

Some of the features embodied by the iconography elucidate possibilities of transcending beyond the rigid restriction of the representative discourse of otherness. If the familiarity with foreigners created initial images of stereotype, these images were representative of the scope of elements used in the depiction of daily life of Theban subjects. Such images provide the possibility to read these representations as human projections through the dynamism of society, being pervaded by the official power and by the agency of the subalterns. Consequently, if 'there is no escape from the politics of representation' (Hall 2013, 384), not even the representation is immune to itself.

References

Anthony, F. B. 2017. **Foreigners in Ancient Egypt: Theban Tomb Paintings from the Early Eighteenth Dynasty**. London: Bloomsbury.

Arrais, N. 2011. **Os Feitos Militares nas Biografias do Reino Novo: Ideologia Militarista e Identidade Social sob a XVIIIª Dinastia do Egito Antigo 1550–1295 a. C**. Unpublished PhD Dissertation. Niterói: Universidade Federal Fluminense.

Barth, F. 2011. Grupos Étnicos e suas Fronteiras. In P. Poutignat, J. Streiff-Fenart ed. **Teorias da Etnicidade**. São Paulo: Editora da Unesp, 187–227.

Bhabha, H. 2013. **O Local da Cultura**. Belo Horizonte: Editora da UFMG.

Bianchi, R. 2004. **Daily Life of the Nubians**. Westport: Greenwood Press.

Bourdieu, P. 1989. **O Poder Simbólico**. Rio de Janeiro: Bertrand Brasil.

Bourdieu, P. 1996. **A Economia das Trocas Lingüísticas**. São Paulo: EDUSP.

Costa, S. 2006. Desprovincializando a Sociologia: a Contribuição Pós-Colonial. **Revista Brasileira de Ciências Sociais**, 21(60), 117–183.

Champollion, J. 1833. **Lettres écrites d'Égypte et de Nubie en 1828 et 1829**. Paris: Firmin Didot.

Dabbs, G. and S. Zakrzewski. 2011. Craniometric Variation at Tell el- Amarna: Egyptians or Interlopers at the "Heretic King's" City? **American Journal of Physical Anthropology**, 144, Supp. S52, 119.

Dabbs, G., J. C. Rose and M. Zabecki. 2015. The Bioarchaeology of Akhetaten: Unexpected Results from a Capital City. In S. Ikram, J. Kaiser and R. Walker eds. **Egyptian Bioarchaeology: Humans, Animals, and the Environment**. Leiden: Sidestone Press, 43–52.

Davies, N. de G. and A. Gardiner. 1926. **The Tomb of Huy: Viceroy of Nubia in the Reign of Tutankhamun**. London: The Egypt Exploration Society.

Davies, N. de G. and A. Gardiner. 1936. **Ancient Egyptian Paintings**. Vol. 1. Chicago: University of Chicago Press.

Emerit, S. 2013. Music and Musicians. In E. Frood, W. Wendrich eds. **UCLA Encyclopedia of Egyptology**. Los Angeles: UCLA, 1–16.

Geertz, C. 1989. **A Interpretação das Culturas**. Rio de Janeiro: LTC Editora.

Given, M. 2005. **The Archaeology of the Colonized**. London: Routledge.

Grimal, N. 2005. **A History of Ancient Egypt**. Oxford: Blackwell Publishing.

Hall, S. 2013. **Da Diáspora: Identidades e Mediações Culturais**. Belo Horizonte: Editora UFMG.

Kemp, B. J. 1979. Imperialism and Empire in New Kingdom Egypt. In P. D. A. Garnsey and C. R. Whittaker ed. **Imperialism in the Ancient World**. Cambridge: Cambridge University Press, 7–58.

Kemp, B. J. 2006. **Ancient Egypt: Anatomy of a Civilization**. London: Routledge.

Loprieno, A. 2012. Slavery and Servitude. In E. Frood, W. Wendrich eds. **UCLA Encyclopedia of Egyptology**. Los Angeles: UCLA, 1–19.

Meskell, L. 2004. **Object Worlds in Ancient Egypt**. Oxford: Berg.

Mokhtar, G. and J. Vercoutter. 1983. Introdução Geral. In G. Mokhtar org. **História Geral da África – A África Antiga**. São Paulo: Ática, XXXI-LXII.

Morkot, R. 2000. **The Black Pharaohs: Egypt's Nubian Rulers**. London: Rubicon.

Navrátilová, H. and Malek, J. eds. 2012. **Theban Tomb Tracings Made by Norman and Nina de Garis Davies**. The Griffith Institute - University of Oxford.

O'Connor, D. 1983. New Kingdom and Third Intermediate Period. In B. Trigger, B.J. Kemp, D. O'Connor and A.B. Lloyd. **Ancient Egypt: a Social History**. Cambridge: Cambridge University Press, 183–278.

Riggs, C. and J. Baines. 2012. Ethnicity. In E. Frood, W. Wendrich eds. **UCLA Encyclopedia of Egyptology**. Los Angeles: UCLA, 1–16.

Säve-Söderbergh, T. and L. Troy. 1991. **New Kingdom Pharaonic Sites: the Finds and the Sites** Partille: Paul Åström.

Smith, S. 2003. **Wretched Kush: Ethnic Identities and Boundaries in Egypt's Nubian Empire**. London: Routledge.

Smith, S. 2007. Ethnicity and Culture. In T. Wilkinson ed. **The Egyptian World**. London: Routledge, 218–241.

Török, L. 2009. **Between Two Worlds: the Frontier Region Between Ancient Nubia and Egypt – 3700 BC–500 AD**. Leiden: Brill.

Wilkinson, C. K. and M. Hill. 1983. **Egyptian Wall Paintings: The Metropolitan Museum's Collection of Facsimiles**. New York: The Metropolitan Museum of Art.

The authors

Érika Maynart (erikarmramos@gmail.com) received her MPhil in Social History from the Universidade de São Paulo (USP), where she is currently a research associate in the Laboratory of the Ancient Near East.

Carolina Velloza (carolina.velloza@hotmail.com) received her MPhil in Social History from the Universidade de São Paulo (USP), where she is a research associate in the Laboratory of the Ancient Near East. In 2016, she was awarded a fellowship at the École du Louvre and worked in the Département des Antiquités Égyptiennes of the Musée du Louvre.

Rennan Lemos (rdsl3@cam.ac.uk) is a Cambridge Trust PhD candidate in Archaeology at Emmanuel College, University of Cambridge. He is currently doing research on New Kingdom cemeteries in Nubia, and is involved in fieldwork in Egypt and Sudan.

Gisela Chapot (gisachapot@gmail.com) received her PhD from the Universidade Federal Fluminense (UFF). She was a visiting student in the Department of Archaeology, University of Cambridge and the Institut für Kunstgeschichte und Archäologie, Rheinische Friedrich-Wilhelms-Universität Bonn. She currently teaches and supervises postgraduate students and is a postdoctoral research associate in the Laboratory of Egyptology of Museu Nacional, Universidade Federal do Rio de Janeiro.

Benjamin Hinson (b.hinson@vam.ac.uk) received his PhD from the University of Cambridge. He is now assistant curator in the Asian Department of the Victoria and Albert Museum, London.

Uroš Matić (urosmatic@uni-muenster.de) received his PhD from the Universität Münster. He is a DAAD postdoctoral fellow at the Institut für Orientalische und Europäische Archäologie, Österreichischen Akademie der Wissenschaften and the Institut für Ägyptologie und Koptologie, Universität Münster.

Carmen Muñoz Pérez (carmen.mun.per@gmail.com) is a PhD candidate at the École du Louvre and the Université Paul-Valéry Montpellier 3, where she is part of Égypte Nilotique et Méditerranéenne (UMR 5140 – Archéologie des Sociétés Méditerranéennes). Her research focuses on amulets and their relationship with funerary practices based on the collection of the Département des Antiquités Égyptiennes of the Musée du Louvre.

Marcelo Rede (mrede@usp.br) is a lecturer in ancient history at the Universidade de São Paulo, where he is a member of the Laboratory of the Ancient Near East. He received his PhD in Assyriology from the Université Paris 1 Panthéon-Sorbonne. He is a research associate in the UMR 7041 Archéologie et Sciences de l'Antiquité/Histoire et Archéologie de l'Orient Cunéiforme. He has published extensively on the economic history of Mesopotamia, including the unpublished documents from Tell Senkereh (Larsa).

Fábio Amorim Vieira (fabioamorimvieira@gmail.com) received his MPhil in History from the Universidade Federal do Rio Grande do Sul (UFRGS). He is a research associate in the Laboratory of Postcolonial and Decolonial Studies, Universidade do Estado de Santa Catarina (UDESC).